FROM **FRUSTRATED**
TO
Frickin' Awesome!

Carolin,

You are frickin'
awesome!! Keep unlocking
+ unleashing your
superpowers!

♡ Alex

FROM **FRUSTRATED**
TO
Frickin' Awesome!

4 Steps to Achieve the Success You're Wired For

Alissa Daire Nelson

Strengths Strategy Certified Coach &
Host of *Maximize Your Strengths* Podcast

www.alissadairenelson.com
www.strengthspodcast.com
www.daire2succeed.com
ISBN: 1543015530
ISBN 13: 9781543015539
Library of Congress Control Number: 2017902052
CreateSpace Independent Publishing Platform
North Charleston, South Carolina
Edits: Cari Twitchell & Jeff Coughenour
Cover design: Heather Coughenour
Photos: Laine Torres Photography

Dedication

To my beautiful daughters, Avery and Annika. Your futures are filled with bright and amazing successes as well as a few painful failures. Remember in all moments that you are inexplicably valuable and indescribably awesome. May you grow to be confident and proud of how you are wired. My wish for you is to grow into better versions of you each day. I love you to the moon!

Contents

Acknowledgments

They say it takes a village to raise a child. In all things, in all accomplishments, it takes a village.

This book would not have come into fruition without a slew of people who care about me. I am humbled and so, so grateful.

To Joel, my rock. Your calm, undying support in all things kept me breathing throughout this entire process. Your belief in me, even when my belief in myself wavered, kept me strong and moving forward. Thank you for being the man by my side, leading me into success with your hand on the small of my back.

To Beth, my kriger; to Cari, my priority queen, focuser, and brain-sorter; to Heather, my bright-and-shining creative blue thunder; and, to Jeff, my gentle, patient, analytical voice. You four are always there. Period. You are more than friends. You are the definition of what selfless giving looks like. Without you, I very likely would have given up on the dream of writing this book. Thank you for working as hard on this project as I did. I would cross oceans for you. I can't describe how much I love and appreciate you.

To John Lee Dumas, you lit the fire, my friend. Your Freedom Journal and the challenge (and promise) that great things can happen in 100 days inspired me to write this book. Your unyielding belief and encouragement means the world to me.

To DeAnna Murphy, your expansive and abundant view on life, Strengths, and humanity, is inspiring. You lead by example always and I'm eternally grateful for the unique and beautiful light you've brought to the Strengths world and to my life. I would not be the woman I am without your influence. Thank you.

Preface

Hey there! Thank you so much for taking the time to pick up this book and share your time with me. I really am looking forward to spending the time with you, too, and can't wait to connect with you after you read this! My name is Alissa Daire Nelson and I'm a Strengths Strategy Certified Coach. I'd like to share a little about who I am, why I'm writing *this* book in particular, and why I believe you won't regret picking it up.

Starting at the Beginning

I had a good childhood. I had two parents who were committed to raising independent, strong, successful children. But there were seven of us kids. It was sometimes difficult to get noticed, especially with five high-achieving older siblings. Often, the good went unnoticed. The great was acknowledged. And the bad got *a lot* of attention. Straight A's were par for the course, but a C was lecture-worthy.

The focus on the negative was self-driven as well as part of my family culture. I can still vividly remember getting a C in handwriting (of all classes!) when I was in the third grade. The lean of my cursive writing wasn't right-leaning enough, nor did I hold my pencil correctly (yes, this is a true story). Honestly, though, I'm left-handed! What left-handed person do you know that has nice handwriting? None of them! Anyway, I had to practice extra hard. I literally began writing harder; my hand was near black from dragging it through the dark graphite letters. My hand hurt from pressing so hard and so deliberately. My handwriting did get a little better, but not considerably so. I became ashamed of my writing. I only wrote when I had to. To this day, I sometimes feel the twinge of "not-good-enough" when writing a handwritten note.

Weakness Fixing

See, fixing our weaknesses is what our culture promotes. Along with that C in handwriting, I got A's in all other classes, including an A+ in math (I had done extra work above grade level). Those grades didn't get any attention, though. Interesting, right? Regardless of all the good there, the only question I asked myself was, "What's wrong with me?! Why can't I do anything right?" If you've had a similar experience, then you know those feelings and self-talk don't stop with one incident. They continue into other aspects of daily life.

With that culture firmly in place, this is what the first 30 years of my life looked like:

* If I didn't achieve something I set my mind to: "What's *wrong* with me?!"
* If a friend got mad at me: "What's *wrong* with me?!"
* If I didn't get an A in a class: "What's *wrong* with me?!"
* If I felt unsatisfied with the status quo and yearned for change: "What's *wrong* with me?!"

There was always this part of me that felt like everything that went wrong was ultimately my fault and I was somehow innately flawed. But one day, I heard this quote by Mary Kay Ash:

"God didn't have time to make junk."

Whatever your faith base is, there's power in that statement. Ash's comment started a cascade of searching and discovery for me. During my search, I quickly found that I wasn't the only one who defaulted to thinking "What's wrong with me?!" Nearly everyone I spoke to (and I talk to a lot of people; it's my favorite thing!) was struggling with the same thing. They were focused on fixing their weaknesses, trying to overcome flaws, and trying to become "independent" by learning how to be "well-rounded." Most of them were seeking to learn how to be competent in all aspects of their business and life—a Jack of all trades—so they didn't have to ask for help, rely on others, or feel or be perceived as incompetent.

So I set out on a mission to find out who I was. I needed to find out if I was already wired how I was supposed to be. If so, then, dang it, I needed to start embracing it!

Finding Strengths

I read books that felt too good to be true, but I still *wanted* them to be true. I wished and wished for it to come true that I was great, but was always let down in the end. This same journey led me to several coaches, studying NLP (neurolinguistic programming), and then finding the StrengthsFinder®[1] 2.0 profile. StrengthsFinder is based in positive psychology, which looks at the good rather than focusing on the bad. A study that looked at what was *right* with you? Heck yes! I fell in love with the StrengthsFinder philosophy and have since have grown to believe in it as much as gravity.

Here's the truth: You are uniquely made for a unique purpose. No one else is like you. Now it's time for **you** to decide what to do with this knowledge.

---

1 *Copyright© 2017 Gallup, Inc. all rights reserved. Gallup, StrengthsFinder, Clifton StrengthsFinder, and the 34 Clifton StrengthsFinder theme names are trademarks of Gallup, Inc.*

The non-Gallup information has not been approved and is not sanctioned or endorsed by Gallup in any way. Opinions, views and interpretations of Clifton StrengthsFinder are solely the beliefs of Alissa Daire Nelson and Daire Success Coaching.

Introduction

If I would've had this book when I started out—not just in the entrepreneurial space, but as a teen or young adult—I would have been able to make *better* decisions, *more confidently*, and would have been able to *relish* in my differences rather than hide or fix them. I would have started the process earlier of developing self-grace and self-worth. It would have helped me understand that I am not a "lesser form" of someone else, but that my uniqueness is real and is frickin' awesome.

Founded in Logic

I like proof. I do also believe in the spiritual realm and understand there are things that are unseen, but also true. Still, I have always wanted to know that there's a reason my brain works the way it does. I needed everything physiologically explained, as it's easier for me to accept things when there's *proof*.

I get so angry when I hear some "expert" blowing smoke and telling you that if you *believe* hard enough, your dreams will come true. I hear so much of this crap! "If it doesn't happen, it wasn't meant to be," or "just attract what you're looking for into your life and it will come." Bleh. This is about grounding ourselves in objectivity, dreaming big, and getting your butt into action to *back those dreams up.*

I realize they may sound cynical. But if you've been let down by this approach in the past, I'm betting you turned it on yourself:

> "I didn't pray hard enough."
> "My dreams must be just a figment of my imagination. I'll never be great."
> Oh! Here it is again! "What's *wrong* with me?! I let myself down *again.*"

Ready for more logic? Here you go, whether you want it or not. There is a reason—a fundamental, animal-kingdom reason—that you cannot do everything on your own. Sure, scientifically, there are certain animal species that live independently. Human beings, however, are *not* one of those species. We require community. We *thrive* in community.

My goal with this book is to provide a logical foundation for solo business owners and business partners who believe they have to do it all on their own. And, further, they believe they are failures if they cannot succeed on their own.

Know You Are Enough

You've tried positive affirmations. You even posted those affirmations on your bathroom mirror and refrigerator. But, somehow, they didn't work, and you gave up on them. You still feel like you're scrambling to just stay above water. You're running a rat race. You're tired. You may even feel defeated, and you certainly feel frustrated.

Let me start by saying this:

You are enough.

Moreover, I will prove it to you in this book. I will help you realize you have a distinctive place here. In fact, you will come to see you have a *responsibility* to be your best and to share your best with the world.

By the end of this (intentionally) short, actionable book, you will have an amazing breakthrough about what your unique selling proposition really is, give up Imposter Syndrome, spend more of your time in tasks and areas that give you energy instead of sucking it out of you, and put wishful thinking away for good. You will have a four-step process that you can repeat with better results each time. When the temptation arises to "compare and despair," you will have tools to bring you back to the truth and allow you to take action.

When we are done here, you will see that *you are actually awesome.* Legit. Backed by science, facts, and positive psychology. And you'll be able to act on that awesomeness.

Rest assured that this book won't turn you into an arrogant jerk. Your air of awesomeness will come from a place of **confidence**—not conceit. You'll delight in knowing that you are not someone else, or even a mishmash of a bunch of someone else's. You will be happy for everyone else, too, and will come to see even your stiffest competition in a different light.

How to Use This Book

I spend my days coaching solo entrepreneurs, business partners, and teams to find their sweet spots, get unstuck, and break through barriers that keep them from reaching their greatest potential and maximum synergy. And while the process and strategy of getting things done and running a business is vital to success, which I will also talk about, 90 percent of the work happens before we even consider the busyness of our business. Without uncovering and accepting how you tick and what makes you awesome, you'll easily lose your way, get and remain discouraged, self-sabotage, and fall short of your true potential. The work in this book is your insurance policy for success.

It is normal to get stuck when you hit a roadblock or cross-roads. It's normal to find yourself exhausted sometimes. The question is how long will you stay there?

Who Should Read This Book?

Ultimately, there are three different types of people that will benefit from this book:

> The self-confident person who somehow can't figure out why success has eluded them.
> The creative person who has a glimmer of hope that somewhere, deep within, they've got what it takes, but is unsure if their idea is *good enough* to really make a difference.
> The shy, humble, and sweet woman who has shrunk away from the limelight because she doesn't want to be viewed as selfish or arrogant.

While these types sound very different, they have a few things in common. Each of them is *frustrated* with their current place in life and business. They've got pieces of the success puzzle, but haven't quite put it together yet. Each has failed at following "guaranteed plans" for success and happiness in the past; they are beginning to wonder if their experiences just confirm that *they* are the problem.

Because here's the deal. It's not enough to know that you're frickin' awesome. And it's not enough to have a plan and take action. **You need both**.

If you're ready to stop spinning your wheels and start spiraling *up*, this is the book for you.

What This Book Is Not

This is not a sales tactics book. While the art of selling is worth learning, without personal development you will achieve only short-lived success.

Here's a baseline fact about selling: People buy from people they like. You will never have the opportunity to pitch your products or services if you're not first authentically connecting to your potential client. That said, for them to know, like, and trust you, you must know, like, and trust yourself.

By the way, I am not saying that learning how to sell properly isn't important. Absolutely read up on proper sales techniques and tactics. If you're looking for good recommendations, I am personally fond of these books:

* Daniel Pink's "To Sell Is Human"
* Zig Ziglar's "Secrets of Closing the Sale"
* Dale Carnegie's "How to Win Friends and Influence People"

But read this book first. Know yourself before you try to emulate someone else's sales tactics. Following a plan is smart and can guide your way, but it needs to be tweaked to fit *you*.

Also, this book is not based on wishful or delusional thinking. Mindset and positivity are powerful. They also have scientific evidence to back up their legitimate influence in your success. But I have seen people set goals and create expectations for themselves that are, by any measure, impossible (at least in the timeframe they set). They use phrases like, "You've got to think bigger to achieve more!" and "It doesn't matter that this has never been achieved before. I can do *anything* I set my mind to!"

Take this quote by the great Jean-Luc Picard from "Star Trek: The Next Generation":

"Things are impossible only until they're not."

This is so true! I love a future-thinking, hope-filled, record-breaking story as much as the next person. But you won't go from zero to a million dollars overnight. You won't go from beginner to expert in a year, especially if your only plan is to "work really hard." Create your goals with a realistic game plan. Eat the elephant one bite at a time, as the saying goes. Pretty soon, you *will* achieve the impossible; you just don't get to teleport there overnight.

Finally, while the information I provide here *is* breakthrough, it is not a magic pill. *There is no magic pill.*

There is no "breakthrough of all breakthroughs," because following each breakthrough comes a new level of challenge.

That's a good thing! Embrace each mini-breakthrough you have, and accept that you will face challenges throughout the process. With this book in hand, you will be better prepared to face those challenges. You can continually come back here to recall, recalibrate, and reassess all of what makes you amazing. Consider this book your homing beacon for self truth.

This book will not "fix" you. In fact, I'll go even further and say that you don't *need* to be fixed. It will not magically remove all of your doubts and fears. But it *will* show you the truth. And knowing the truth will free you to blow past those doubts and fears.

This is not a one-and-done process. You will have doubts. Your negative self-talk might get loud. Disappointments and negative feedback from others (whether true or simply intended to tear you down) will cause a hitch in your step. You will get stuck from time to time. And you will have moments when you have no idea how to move forward. That is why it is so important that you have this book.

If you are looking for a positive approach to setting yourself apart from the crowd and building momentum to your success quarter over quarter, you're in the right place. If you are ready to dig in and prove to yourself why your competition is irrelevant … If you are ready to begin soaring … Let's go!

Chapter 1

●　●　●

Realizing the Truth:
You're Already Awesome

(And why you haven't found your sweet spot yet)

I'm frickin' awesome!

ALISSA DAIRE NELSON

t took me over 30 years to be able to say, "I am awesome,"
and believe it. This means I spent the first three decades of
my life struggling to earn my value. I never relished in what I
was, the talents I was born with, or my personality. I thought
that "success" was *improving* all of that. And by improving, I
mean changing it all. I also believed that I needed to prove my
worth. But what a yo-yo! This meant every time I achieved

something, it validated my worth. And every time I failed at something or screwed up, it was proof that I was flawed.

When I looked at others, I saw all of their great attributes. What did I see in me? All the negatives. It was like I was blind to the good things! Sure, I felt good when I accomplished something and was praised for it. But I didn't feel good just "being." My focus was on my "flaws," not on what makes me unique and great. Can you relate?

So it's an incredible accomplishment for me to say out loud with confidence "I really like me!" My husband usually laughs when I say something like that and comes back with, "Well, there's your modesty coming out again!" But here's the deal. I AM awesome! HE is awesome. And YOU are frickin' awesome. We are "fearfully and wonderfully made."[2]

By the time you finish this book and the exercises in it, I want to hear you say and believe, "I'm *actually* awesome!" And when you realize it, I want you to tweet me @daire2succeed. Tell me what makes you awesome and use the hashtag **#iamawesome.** Remember, I want you to mean it from the core of your soul!

Does simply reading that request make your heart beat faster? Are these questions now circling around in your brain:

---

2   *The Bible. The New Revised Standard Version, Psalm 139:14, 1993.*

"What if people criticize me?" "What if I'm wrong?" "What if people think I'm arrogant?"

Look, recognizing what is awesome and why you are different from everyone else has absolutely nothing to do with arrogance. Instead, it has everything to do with self-worth. You can't expand the gifts you have and the natural talents you were born with until you accept their existence in the first place!

Let's quickly review what the common current model is for setting ourselves apart. Then we'll dive into the "Frickin' Awesome" process.

The Current Sales Model for Setting Yourself Apart Doesn't Work

"The customer is *always* right."

This is the phrase you hear to promote "great customer service." Using this method you inevitably feel like you have to bend over backward and sacrifice your own sanity and/or self-respect to make the customer happy. And, consequently, you're stuck with the precedent that you'll do *anything* to make people happy. Congratulations! You're now a doormat.

"We'll beat any advertised price!"
"You'll never see prices this low."

You might be able to win a sale once by offering up a discount, but unless you have another way of winning loyalty, getting clients through the door isn't going to automatically set you up for repeat sales. People will stop buying your product or service at full price. They will believe the true value of what you're selling *is* the sale price, and they come off believing that selling something at full price is simply price gouging.

"You'll never find this anywhere else."

Another sales tactic that people often use to set themselves apart is making big promises and guarantees to their future clients and customers. Even if your promise isn't intended to be a lie, you always lose if you make promises you can't keep or guarantees you can't stand behind.

> **A short caveat:** Making a mistake is *not* the same as deceit. You *will* make mistakes and you *will* fall short. But who you are and how you handle those mistakes can mean everything to salvaging a spectacular relationship with your clients.

Setting Yourself Apart the Right Way: A Case Study

Oftentimes we think of ourselves as not being able to compete with the "big guys." Really, how could a mom-and-pop convenience store possibly compete with Walmart?

They can, and here's why: They don't have to be Walmart's competition. Walmart may undercut prices nearly every single time, but what else are they offering their customers? What will you offer your customers that would create loyalty and make them choose you over Walmart in the future?

Three years ago, a big-box wine and liquor store opened up one-half-mile from Fairview Wine & Spirits in Roseville, Minnesota. Steve Burwell, who opened Fairview Wine & Spirits in 1985, sat down with me to explain how this little mom-and-pop liquor store "competed" with the big-box store.

While he was understandably shaken when that store opened, Steve knew they weren't selling the same thing:

> "We sell convenience, service, knowledge, and friendliness. We treat people how we would want to be treated. I'm a nice guy. I'm sincere. The people who come in here are like my family. I know their names, their kids, their jobs".

Steve's passion is obvious: customer service and relationships. *That's the bottom line.* So who shops at his liquor store? All the people he's created relationships with during the last 30-plus years. All the people, myself included, who share his values of caring for people and a familiar, friendly face. All the people that trust him and his employees' knowledge of all things spirits and wine. Anyone who appreciates being educated and sold on a $25 bottle of wine that is the same quality and flavor as a $90 bottle. And all the people who value relationships and an authentic smile over saving a buck or two off a national-brand beer.

See, Steve didn't worry about the *one* thing (those basement prices on some items) that he couldn't offer. Instead, he focused on what he was good at, what set him apart. He didn't waver from his values, strengths, or commitments. In fact, he leaned into them more.

That big-box store isn't competition for Steve of Fairview Wine & Spirits. It doesn't even come close.

Chapter 2

The Strategic Grind

It takes time. It's a grind. There are no
shortcuts. You've got to grind and grind.

MARK CUBAN

I am a fan of hard work. In fact, I believe hard work, sacrifice, and failure are all parts of success.

There is no overnight success. Why? Because success is the achievement of something you once had not achieved, i.e. if it was easy, everyone would do it (and it wouldn't be considered a success).

Whatever your measure of success, know it takes work. It requires making difficult choices rather than taking the easy way out. And it requires learning. You learn best from doing, *experiencing*. You can save yourself the pain of failing by... Never. Doing. Anything. But you'll also lose out on incredible fulfillment, achievements, and adventures. So, change your view on failure. It gives you a chance to learn. Then become obsessed with learning.

Success is not strictly about metrics. You cannot reach the pinnacle of success simply by making more calls, going to more networking meetings, or sending more emails. Does all of this increase your chances? Heck yes! But *only if* you're willing to let every call, every email, and every interaction be an opportunity to learn, hone, and master your craft … and you do it with your best foot forward.

By all means, make those calls, send those emails, and attend those meetings. Do lots of all of those things! But do them in alignment with your values. Sacrifice, but don't sacrifice your character or your values. ***Emulate* a mentor, but be you**. Here's why:

> If you try to follow someone else's exact formula without considering who you are and what you have that's uniquely you, you'll be frustrated, exhausted, and you will wonder why "the proven system" didn't work for you.

The typical grind usually includes making the same mistakes over and over again. It involves going through the motions, being hyper-focused on fixing your weaknesses, and beating yourself up in the comparison game.

I promise you this: There *is* another way, and I will show it to you.

Performance Matters

Performance *does* matter. It's not enough to say, "I'm not innately talented at data-entry or analyzing numbers," and then not do your books. It's not enough to say, "I'm not a people person," and then ignore the relationships you have with your customers.

Identifying your innate talents and Strengths is not a free pass to ignore your weaknesses. It's not an excuse to leave your innate talents undeveloped. You owe it to yourself and your current customers to strive for excellence and to put the work in that produces results. *Performance matters.*

Three Paths to Excellence

You can achieve excellence in performance in one of three ways:

1. **Sharpen a talent into a Strength.** This is fun and energizing. It also takes work (because anything worthwhile takes an investment of time and energy).
2. **Sharpen an area of non-talent.** This is possible, but it takes considerable energy and time, as well as

drudgery, angst, and even more energy and time. This is *not* fun, it sucks the energy right out of you, and is painful. But, again, it is possible.

3. **Surround yourself with people who are better than you at the things you don't have talent in.** Sometimes this means you pay them to do what they are good at. Sometimes you collaborate and you benefit mutually from the areas you are each good at. And, sometimes, it's a combination of the two.

If you are like most folks, you were brought up with the belief of "no pain, no gain." So, somehow, option number two above seems like it would produce the results you are looking for because it *hurts* more than the others. Don't fall into this trap.

Also, if you're bootstrapped, how do you afford the luxury of outsourcing what you're not good at, as described in option number three? Valid question. Unfortunately, there is no cut-and-dried answer. But here is the best rule of thumb I can share: If you have more time than money, do it yourself. If you have more money than time, hire it out.

So, what if you're strapped for time *and* you have no additional funds? You are not alone; many entrepreneurs are in your shoes. If this is you, you *must* find collaborative relationships. Such relationships can absolutely bring success, but how you set them up is important. Trading services is quite common.

And nearly 100 percent of the time, it's a disaster. All too often one of the parties ends up feeling they were taken advantage of or gave more than the other.

To make this a win-win-win (good for you, them, *and* the situation), both parties need to legitimately benefit from each other's services/products. And providing invoices to each other will keep your minds clear on what each is doing for the other. These situations tend to have scope creep (when additional "just-one-more-thing" tasks or continuous growth in a project's scope occurs) on one or both sides, and the waters get muddied. Collaborate, but keep things professional and expectations clear.

It's possible you have a friend or spouse who is willing to help *and* who has skills and talents that bring great benefits. They love you and want you to succeed. Take the help with massive doses of gratitude and give back with your own talents in service to them.

One of the things you'll learn and embrace in this book is that you were never meant to be "independent" in the first place, so getting clear on *how* you'll collaborate or enter into Interdependence is part of setting yourself apart. You'll need to know (and you'll discover here) what talents and Strengths you *do* have, as well as which ones you don't, before you can seek out others to fill in your gaps, or non-strengths.

Hope for a Better Way

There is a better way, and I will show it to you throughout the remainder of this book. Here is what you can expect to find as you move forward with me.

In Chapters 4-7, you'll learn how to self-elicit all of the things that make you great (Step 1 of the "Frickin' Awesome" process). I'll guide you through exercises that will define your values, important life experiences, education, and your innate talents. You'll discover that you are truly and legitimately awesome. And we'll talk about how you can *actually* embrace it.

In Chapters 8-10, you'll learn how to plan and practice your personal greatness. You'll learn how to get and stay in your Zone of Genius more and more. You'll be able to tailor your approach to planning and carrying out your goals (Step 2) in a way that energizes you (Step 3) and honors how you're uniquely wired. The "doing" will energize you, instead of suck you dry.

In Chapters 12-14, you'll learn the tools required to maintain and grow the newly uncovered you. You've laid the groundwork, but how will you continue? How will you "stay on the wagon?" How will you not just keep the ball rolling, but gain momentum? The answers to these questions are here. You will learn how to evaluate what you've done (Step 4) to *build* on that over and over.

You *can* be awesome. In fact, **you already are**. Your awesomeness is in you, waiting to be found, cultivated, and maximized. Your breakthrough lies just ahead. Ready? Set? It's time to peel away from the pack and find your own path.

Chapter 3

●　　●　　●

Taking a Strengths-Based Approach

Your weaknesses will never develop,
while your Strengths will develop infinitely.

DR. DONALD O. CLIFTON

A large part of my coaching practice, and thus much of this book, centers on the StrengthsFinder® 2.0 profile. I love the StrengthsFinder so much. It's incredibly well studied (40 years of research before it was ever released, and the research continues 17 years later). Now, I am not a statistician or a researcher, but I *must* have real data to support assertions such as, "You're one of a kind!"

The Clifton StrengthsFinder (which I'll refer to as CSF from here on out) is a psychometric tool. This means it is a studied, objective measurement of skills, knowledge, abilities, attitudes, personality traits, and educational achievement. This is important because it means you can trust the results.

What does the CSF tell you? It identifies the areas (Themes) in which you have the greatest aptitude or capacity to grow and excel. It's like having an insider's track on which horse is going to win the race. This blueprint will affirm some things you already knew about yourself and will bring understanding and awareness that might just blow your mind.

A Note About Weaknesses

This book is based in reality, remember? Realizing you're awesome the way you are wired does not mean that you are ignoring your weaknesses. Neither are you using your Strengths to "cop out" on bad habits, inefficient or poorly functioning behaviors, and claiming, "Nothing I can do! I'm just wired this way!" Nope.

Fixed vs. Growth Mindsets

To assume you are stuck with what Strengths and non-Strengths you have *in their current form*, and that there is no room to grow, adapt, or learn, is all part of living with a fixed mindset. In her book, "Mindset: The New Psychology of Success," Stanford University psychology researcher Carol Dweck describes the fixed mindset:

"In a fixed mindset [people] believe their basic abilities, their intelligence, their talents, are just fixed traits, [set in stone]. They have a certain amount and that's that, and then their goal becomes to look smart all the time and never look dumb."

Some people, at first glance, believe that CSF is a prescription (or excuse) to believe in the fixed mindset. Quite the opposite is true. CSF is all about defining where you are naturally talented, and then growing and developing those areas. The growth of your CSF Themes is vital living a fulfilling and productive life, as is understanding your areas of non-Strength. According to Dweck, a growth mindset includes:

"Viewing potential as ability to grow and develop through hard work, practice or progressive improvement; ability is a starting point that can grow. Growth is nurtured through recognition of all learning and motivation to shift, explore and to leave outcomes open-ended."

So, let's just call it out. You do not have all 34 CSF Themes of Strength in equality, nor can you develop them all into Strengths. By default, this means you are naturally better at some things and some ways of thinking than others. You also have weaknesses. But how much do they matter? And what is a weakness anyway? I have a couple definitions for you to consider.

According to Dictionary.com, "weakness" is:

1. The state or quality of being weak; lack of strength, firmness, vigor, or the like; feebleness.
2. An inadequate or defective quality, as in a person's character; slight fault or defect.

DeAnna Murphy of Strengths Strategy provides another definition. She says weaknesses come from three areas:[3]

1. Blind spots or areas of non-Strength—the places we lack perspective, knowledge, or skill.
2. Overuse of our Strengths—the times when our Strengths are working "too hard" or are dialed up too loud.
3. Underuse of our Strengths—the times when we can't or don't use our Strengths to serve ourselves or others.

The *biggest* area of our weaknesses, approximately two-thirds, come from our Strength Talents misapplied!

Well, isn't that lovely? How are you supposed to know the difference between a weakness and a misapplied strength? Here is the simple litmus test: Each CSF Theme is only a

---

3 *Murphy, DeAnna. Strengths Strategy. "How Weaknesses Strengthen Relationships". www.strengthsstrategy.com/2015/02/13/weakness-strengthens-relationships. Accessed 11 Nov 2016.*

Strength when **it gives life to you and it gives life to others**. Gauge that, and you'll know.

You're Not Wired to Be Well Rounded

Understand that who you're wired to be is the raw, "talented," version of you. You can grow, sharpen, and mold your talents into Strengths.

A beginning, but talented, gymnast isn't ready for the Olympics. Without training; overcoming obstacles, challenges, and setbacks; and maintaining a commitment to the end goal, she doesn't reach gold on the Olympic podium. Likewise, you were not "born ready." You continue to develop into a better version of yourself as you work on developing who you already are.

There's a Bible parable that tells a tale of three men.[4] They were each given money, which the story called talents, by their boss. (I love that they were called talents!) Two of them took the money and doubled it by investing, trading, and doing business. The third took his talent and buried it in the ground. He did nothing with it and the boss chastised him. Why? Because when you are given talents and choose to do nothing with them, you are, in fact, squandering them. It is your *responsibility* to develop and grow your innate talents.

---

4   *The Bible. The New Revised Standard Version, Matthew 25: 14-30, 1993.*

On Your Mark

We've laid a lot of groundwork, and now I ask that you open yourself up to the truth that *you are already awesome*. Bruises, warts, stretch marks, and all (physical, spiritual, and emotional).

In his acceptance speech for the Best Actor Oscar in 2014, Matthew McConaughey outlined what I want for you. In thoughtful response to the question, "Who is your hero?" a fifteen-year-old Matthew replied:

> "'You know who it is? It's me in 10 years.' So I turned 25. Ten years later, that same person comes to me and says, 'So, are you a hero?' And I was like, 'Not even close. No, no, no.' She [inquired further], 'Why?' I said, 'Because my hero's me at 35.' So, you see, every day, every week, every month, and every year of my life, my hero's always 10 years away. I'm never gonna be my hero. I'm not gonna attain that. I know I'm not, and that's just fine with me because that keeps me with somebody to keep on chasing."

You don't need to **fix** you. You need to **grow** who you already are. Chase your future you. Start chasing today.

Chapter 4

●　●　●

Uncovering What Makes You Unique

God didn't have time to make a nobody,
only a somebody.

MARY KAY ASH

We all have opinions and beliefs about ourselves, both limiting and empowering. We have a stack of opinions about others, too, right? This person is a "good" person; That person is a "bad" person. Some opinions come from discernment (what you believe is right and wrong) and others come from your inner empowering and limiting belief system—your self-judgment, self-esteem, or self-worth.

Often self-esteem and self-worth are used interchangeably, but Dr. Christina Hibbert describes their differences succinctly and simply:[5]

> "*Self-esteem* is what we think and feel and believe about ourselves. *Self-worth* is recognizing, 'I am greater than all of those things.' It is a deep knowing that I am of value, that I am loveable, necessary to this life, and of incomprehensible worth. It is possible to feel 'high self-esteem,' or in other words, to *think* I'm good at something, yet still not feel *convinced* that I am loveable and worthy. Self-esteem doesn't last or 'work' without self-worth."

The activities in this chapter are designed to move you forward in the growth of your **self-worth**. Many of us were taught that our self-worth is based on our accomplishments and production. While it's important to contribute to society on a whole, I want you to know that *regardless* of what you have or have not done up to this point, you are indescribably valuable!

---

5 *Hibbert, Dr. Christina. "Self-Esteem vs. Self-Worth: Q & A with Dr. Christina Hibbert [plus video]". www.drchristinahibbert.com/self-esteem-vs-self-worth. Accessed 20 September, 2016.*

Once your self-worth is firmly intact, no obstacle can keep you from achieving amazing things! So, are you game to uncover and embrace your true self-worth, even if it means getting uncomfortable? Good. Let's get to work! This chapter is going to require a pen and notebook, so take a moment now to grab those; I'll wait right here.

There are four areas we're going to work on in this section: 1) values, morals, and beliefs; 2) experience; 3) education; and 4) your Strengths blueprint.

Values, Morals & Beliefs

> *It's not hard to make decisions once*
> *you know what your values are.*
>
> Roy E. Disney

Values drive you. Clearly knowing your values is vital. They're what makes you uniquely you. Also, your values change over time, so you should make it a practice to revisit them.

What are values? Your values are your principles or standards of behavior. They are your judgment of what is important in life. Yet, so often, we put our values last. For example, you might say, "My family is the most important thing to me," but they consistently get the last of your attention because your business hijacks your time. You know your family will be there for you while you grind it out. You might say things like, "It's a short-term sacrifice for the long-term gain." Two things:

* The short-term sacrifice is getting longer and longer, and is becoming habit.
* That long-term gain changes and grows, making it one elusive beast.

Now you feel out of balance, guilty, even shameful. You're left wondering, "Is this even worth it?!" You find yourself, more often than not, putting your head on the pillow feeling like you were *busy* all day, but didn't get anything worthwhile done.

I submit to you that I don't believe in balance. I believe in harmony. There are times when you let your personal life creep into work and your work creep into family time. It's virtually impossible to completely compartmentalize all the areas of your life, and doing so takes an *incredible* amount of energy. But if you adopt an attitude of harmony for your life, suddenly your rigid expectations of yourself leave room for grace and flexibility.

If you aren't crystal clear on your values, however, the idea of harmony will get railroaded by a lack of guidelines to help you set boundaries and create priorities.

The first time I ever completed an exercise to elicit my own values, I was working with a coach named Sean Smith, founder of Elite Success Systems.[6] I knew there were things that I "believed in," but hadn't ever written them out. It's now an exercise that I complete with every client because of the power and clarity it provides. I'd like to complete it with you now.

Take Action: This is most powerful when completed with a partner, but can be done on your own in a pinch. An important caveat here is that your partner *must* come into the exercise with no judgment. You need to be able to share without fearing criticism.

---

6 *Smith, Sean. www.coachseansmith.com.*

Values Exercise

Step 1: Make Your Raw List

1) Grab your partner, a journal or piece of paper, a pen, and a timer.
2) Set your timer for 5 minutes.
3) Have your partner ask you, "What's important to you?" That's it. That's the only question. He or she will ask you over, and over, and over again. Your partner will write down all the things you say.
4) Answer that question with no more than four or five words at a time.
5) You'll hit spots where you feel like you've run out of things to say, but push through at least two silent spells. Dig deep. *What's really important to you?*
6) After 5 minutes, or multiple silent spells (whichever comes first), your partner will ask you if your list feels complete. If there's anything else you'd like to add to the list, now's the time.

Step 2: Take a Gratitude Break

1) Find a place you can completely relax, sit down, and close your eyes. For five minutes, think grateful thoughts, breathe in gratitude deeply, and bring your awareness and attention to being thankful. Let your

mind's eye look around your brain for all the things you often take for granted, like the ability to walk, electricity that floods a room with light at night with a flip of a switch, a bed to sleep on. All of it. Be grateful for everything.

2) It may help to turn on grateful music during this time. Two suggestions I have are "Blessed" by Martina McBride or "Grateful" by Brotha James. Simply search and listen on YouTube! You can also listen to instrumental music.

Step 3: Re-elicit Your Values

1) Now, repeat Part 1.

2) This time, have your partner ask you, "What's *really* important to you?" The gratitude energy that you created in Step 2 will often allow you to complete your list without any silent or dry spells at all. Again, your partner will write down all of your answers.

3) Use your intuition to know when this part is complete, often within three or four minutes.

Step 4: Combine Similar Values

1) Take your second list and see if any of your answers can be combined. Remember this is *your* list, so how

you interpret each item is up to you. For example, "joy" and "happiness" may or may not be similar or combinable to you, so your partner's role here is to simply ask if values on the list are processed or defined the same. It's not your partner's job to help you define these. This is all about how *you* interpret *your* list.

Step 5: Choose Your Top 10

1) Go through your list and pick out your 10 most important values. (If you have 9 or 11, it's ok. Rigidity isn't the goal here; you just don't want 20 values).
2) Rewrite those Top 10 in alphabetical order. (I recommend you do this in a Word document or other digital format to make Step 6 easier.)

Step 6: Rank Your Values in Order of Importance

Let's say this is your alphabetized list:

Faith
Family
Joy
Leaving a legacy
Meaningful work/contribution
Money
Personal growth

Physical health
Time to myself (quiet time)
Travel/vacation/experiences

1) Your partner will ask you to compare your first two values by asking, "What's more important to you, faith or family?" If your answer is "faith", then your partner's next question is, "What's more important to you, Faith or Joy?" and so on and so forth. (The reason it's best to use a digital format for this part is that you can easily cut and paste as the order becomes clear.)

2) Recognize that this is *hard*. When you get stuck, your partner will ask you, "If you could ONLY have one and not the other, what would it be?" Another way to think about this is, "If I don't have one, can I have the other?" For example, if you didn't have meaningful work, would you be able to leave the legacy that is so important to you? Again, there is no judgment here, including self-judgment. This is your list.

3) Continue down the list, always working downward, until you have one value that is more important than the other nine, then remove it from the questioning and place it at #1.

> Example, you answered "faith" to all nine questions of comparing to the other values, so Faith is your #1 value and your partner moves to,

"What's more important to you, family or joy?" Family.

"What's more important to you, family or leaving a legacy?" Family.

"What's more important to you, family or meaningful work?" Family.

"What's more important to you, family or money?" Family.

So if you answer "family" to eight questions, list family as Value #2 and move on.

"What's more important to you, joy or leaving a legacy?" Leaving a legacy.

"What's more important to you, leaving a legacy or meaningful work?" Meaningful work.

"What's more important to you, meaningful work or money?" …

4) It's normal to have certain values change places when comparing them to values you've already weighed against. Hang in there. You will find the right order. Don't take shortcuts. Often, ranking the top five is the most difficult. The process will speed up as you rank more values. Remember that ranking one over the other does not mean you are saying that one is not important. **All 10 are important.**

Once you have your values in order, you'll be better equipped to make decisions about the priorities in your life. When you reach a crossroad, simply ask yourself, "Does making this decision with my time, attention, or resources honor my values?"

Morals

Morals describe what is right and wrong, while values explain a person's important behavior and beliefs. That's why the values exercise is often a little bit difficult for people. It requires you to rethink your behavior and to align it with your beliefs. For example, you may hold a moral that all people are equally important, so it feels wrong to rank your husband above your children on the values exercise. But the ranking of your values doesn't describe your morals, it guides your behavior. If you believe it's in your kids' best interest to have a healthy relationship with your husband, you will invest time to strengthen your relationship with your husband. This may mean that you arrange to have someone else care for the kids while you and your husband head off to a bed and breakfast for the weekend. You're not saying "my kids are less important" in doing this, you're adjusting your behavior to align with your values.

Let's look at another moral you may hold: Honor your elders. For this reason, it may feel wrong to put "family" lower on the list of values. But remember, your values help guide your behavior. You may decide you need to work rather than take the time to bring your grandmother to the doctor. This doesn't mean you dishonor your grandma, but rather, this is where your time needs to be invested right now. This will guide your conversation with grandma. "I need to finish this important project at work, Grandma, but I'll help find someone who can take you that day."

Life Experience

Life doesn't happen to you, it happens for you.

TONY ROBBINS

Any experience, positive or negative, is part of who you are. Our experiences frame what and how we interpret things and gives us compassion and understanding for others' experiences.

One of my clients experienced terrifying mental, emotional, and physical abuse throughout her entire childhood and into her young adulthood. As you can imagine, she suffers from intense PTSD. On her path to healing, she tried everything. Even with many counselors, therapists, modalities, and medications, nothing helped her substantially. She sought out alternative methods and treatments and didn't give up until she found successful paths for managing her past. Because of her horrific experience, she has an understanding and empathy for others that have gone through trauma. She can listen with a different set of ears, and help others find alternatives and collaborative options to mainstream therapy. She has made it her life's passion to help others heal.

There is no doubt that what happened to her was horrific. It was heartbreaking and unfair and 100 percent not "in God's plan." But she chose to make something good come from her experience.

The sad truth is, you hear stories like this all too often. Another example comes from close to my home. In 1989, 11-year-old Jacob Wetterling was kidnapped. While the Wetterling family was reeling in anguish over the unknown, Jacob's parents, Patty and Jerry, became outspoken activists for child safety. They became key players in the passage and changing of laws to protect children. They became role models and supporters for others going through the same thing. In no way, shape, or form was the abduction of Jacob Wetterling a good thing, but the Wetterlings chose to make good come from it.

Neither my client nor the Wetterlings would ever ask for this to happen to them or to anyone else. But there is value in every negative life experience, and those experiences shape you, guide you, and make you uniquely you.

Positive life experiences also play a role, like being on the high school volleyball team that won state your senior year. Becoming a big brother at age 10, when your parents added a new baby to the family. Hearing story after story of what the Great Depression was *really* like, while learning how to knit from your grandma during your two-week-long summer visits. Learning what close teamwork, gracious winning and losing, and true sportsmanship feel like through being a year-round soccer player for six years as a kid. If your memory sticks with you, write it down; it's important to you.

My parents like to tell a story about me when I was four years old. I apparently loved preschool and was *quite* unhappy when the car didn't start and Mom couldn't bring me to school. So what did four-year-old Alissa do? I snuck out of the side door of the house and *walked there.* I walked two-and-a-half miles, crossing busy streets and all. On my own, I wouldn't have remembered that experience. It not only sheds light on my personality, but also on what my parents thought about me. This translated to how they raised me. And, because they retold that story to me at a young age, it affected what I believed about myself. My mom called me stubborn. My dad called me strong-willed and determined. I learned I could do anything I set my mind to, even if no one else thought I could do it. That experience helped in forming my uniqueness.

You've already had countless experiences in your lifetime, and you'll have countless more. Those experiences are part of what make you uniquely you and enrich what you have to offer.

Take Action: Here's your next assignment. Get your journal or notebook back out.

Experience Exercise

Step 1: Brain Dump

Begin writing down life experiences that made an impression on you. It's often easier to start with negative experiences, as those are the most front of mind (more on why this is later). But don't neglect the positive experiences, too!

Step 2: Phone a Friend

Call someone you knew from childhood. If your parents are living, they're a great option. Or consider calling a sibling or a lifelong friend. Ask them what they remember about you from your childhood. When I did this exercise, I called my oldest sister, who is 10 years my senior. Her vivid experiences helped me see a few of my experiences in a brand new light and gave new insight through memories I had long since forgotten.

Reliving your experiences through someone else's lens can bring memories that you have repressed or forgotten and give you new insight into those experiences.

Step 3: Revisit Your List

Come back to this journal page at least three different times—even better if you're in different moods. You'll come up with different experiences each time.

Step 4: Reflect and Give Thanks

Reflect on these with awe and wonder. Thank each experience for the value it brought to your life, whether it was good or bad. With each, write down one thing you learned through the experience.

Your experiences make you uniquely you and each helps to enrich the person you are.

Education

Education is the most powerful weapon
we can use to change the world.

NELSON MANDELA

We learn through our life experiences. We also learn through formal education.

I believe that no education is ever wasted, and it *always* adds to your depth as a human being and a professional. This holds true even if that education doesn't directly relate to your current career.

Your education includes everything from degrees and certifications to books, seminars, and online courses. I guarantee you have more education than you think you do.

Take Action: Ready for your next exercise? Take that journal or notebook back out and write down as much of your education as you can. You may have success doing this exercise chronologically or topically, so try both!

Education Exercise

Step 1: School

From the beginning of your memory to now, what formal education did you have? What were your extracurricular activities? What electives did you choose and why? Examples:

* Elementary: Violin lessons for 2 years
* Middle School: Took both Spanish and French because Study Hall seemed to be a waste of time
* High School: Joined the choir and took acting lessons to perform in a high school play.
* College, post-college, etc.

Step 2: Certifications

Your "formal" education ends after high school or college. But you and I both know your education doesn't end there. List the certifications, big and small, that you have achieved. Why did you pursue them? What value did they give you?

Step 3: Continuing Education & Seminars

Continuing education credits are useful to remember, too! Even if you are required by state licensure to complete continuing education, typically there is some flexibility in which courses you choose. Why did you choose the ones you did? If certain courses or credits *were* mandated, what did you learn from them?

Repeat this process for all the same reasons for seminars you've attended.

Step 4: Independent Study

What independent study did you complete? What study-from-home courses have you taken? What group coaching or group training programs or courses have you been through? What books have you read? What books have you listened to on Audible?

Are you surprised by how much you were able to include in this section? Impressive! Indeed, your education makes you uniquely you.

Strengths Blueprint

> *What will happen when we think about what is **right** with people rather than fixating on what is **wrong** with them?*
>
> DR. DONALD O. CLIFTON

The final area you need to lock down the fact that you are wonderfully unique is your StrengthsFinder® profile. It all began when psychologist Dr. Clifton asked, "What would happen if we studied what was *right* with people?"

Take Action: This time, sit at your computer so you can dive into your Strengths.

Strengths Exercise

Step 1: Take the Profile

If you've not taken your StrengthsFinder 2.0 profile yet, go to **alissadairenelson.com/profile**. This will redirect you to the Gallup website, where you can invest $15 and 30 minutes to get it![7]

If you have taken the profile, find it and put it in front of you. (I'm willing to bet you didn't know just how much insight your Strengths Profile can give you and you filed it away somewhere.) If you didn't print it out, visit the Gallup website and log into your profile. You will need to know the email address you used to take the profile. If your memory is failing you on that, no big deal. Call Gallup's toll-free number (found on the site); their customer service is quite good and speedy.

Step 2: Learn About Your Strengths

Read the Signature Themes report that Gallup provides you with your CSF profile.

Then subscribe to Maximize Your Strengths Podcast. If you don't have a podcast player on your phone, go to **StrengthsPodcast.com/Strengths**. There, you'll find quick

---

7 *I do not make a commission from CSF profile sales.*

links to all the individual Strengths episodes. Listen to all five episodes for your Top 5. (In iTunes or Stitcher, they are the "All About..." episodes). This will give you a basic understanding of how your Strengths function and thrive.

Step 3: Free Bonus Materials

I've created some great bonus materials that take a deeper dive into Strengths. You can find them at **alissadairenelson.com/bookbonus.**

Chapter 5

● ● ●

Embracing Your Amazingness

Be yourself; everyone else is already taken.

Oscar Wilde

It's one thing to know intellectually that you are really great. It's another thing to actually embrace it.

Your brain is complex. It has been working to make your life, your surroundings, and your decisions make sense, and keep you alive since you were born. About 90% of our brain's function happens subconsciously (with active, conscious effort). It's worth looking at how your brain works so you can take back some control from your subconscious and help your brain work in your favor.

Your Brain's Default State

Kelly McGonigal, health psychologist and author of "The Willpower Effect," explains in her course on self-acceptance what the brain's default state is protective.[8] Your brain is projecting things that aren't true or aren't happening, in part, to protect from future threats. In its downtime, the brain focuses on four main mental activities:

1. **Inner commentary:** Your brain is constantly creating an opinion on the present moment and looking for what is wrong and what can be improved in a type of alternate reality.
2. **Time traveling:** It is thinking about the past or the future, imagined scenarios, and inner fantasies.
3. **Self-referential processing:** It is always creating a sense of self—who you are, "I am the person who ____; I like this and I don't like that; other people should treat me a certain way because of who I am." It defines your identity or ego. This solid, rigid sense of self distances you from others and the present moment.
4. **Social cognition:** Your brain is thinking about others: what they think about you, what you think about them, looking at yourself in relationship to others, and *comparing* yourself to others.

---

8   *McGonigal, Kelly. "Self Acceptance". www.kellymcgonigal.com/ selfacceptance. Accessed 9 Sept 2016.*

So, it turns out that negative self-talk is normal. You are not crazy! But, the reality is that nearly all conjured default-state thoughts are lies. They are worst-case scenarios that your caveman brain is creating to keep you alive, except fear of imminent death isn't really a thing anymore!

The good news is that you *can* counteract this negative default mode. But, you have to be intentional about it.

The Master Sorter- How Your Brain Filters and Chooses Information

Let's dig a little more into how the brain works. Our brain's ultimate job is to filter, sort, and process a ton of information—while the exact numbers vary widely among experts, some say we take in and sort up to two billion bits of information per second to process only about 200 bits of it. In other words, our brain's job is to quickly sort, categorize, and decide which information is necessary to pay attention to.

Ever notice how the first, second, third, and tenth time you visit a place, you notice different things? That's because, the first time, you're soaking it all in and you miss the finer details. But on following visits, your brain quickly scans through the information it's already familiar with and moves to more details.

Our brains have truly amazing capabilities! But this is why I'm telling you this: As the brain creates categories for information, and continues to filter information, it preferentially filters *in* data that confirms beliefs already formed. It essentially seeks more information to confirm existing beliefs, whether or not those beliefs are factual or not. In fact, it will glaze over and filter *out* information that does not support those 'truths'.

Take Little Jack, for example. Little Jack was told he was always going to struggle in school. He couldn't seem to keep up at anything that involved a book. Math, reading, science, ugh! He excelled in sports and made friends easily, but struggled academically. When Jack was 10, he was diagnosed with dyslexia. While the diagnosis was a relief to Jack and his parents, and additional help and tools were offered in school, Jack continued to struggle. He often ended frustrating sessions of homework, with, "See?! I'm just stupid!" No matter that the dyslexia diagnosis helped to "prove" something else was at play, Jack's brain continued to reaffirm the original, early belief that he was "not a smart boy" and glazed over proof that he was, in fact, smart.

Confident Vulnerability

Confident vulnerability is one of my most favorite concepts. I learned it from my mentor, DeAnna Murphy, President and CEO of Strengths Strategy, Inc. And she has this say about the concept of Confident Vulnerability:[9]

---

9 *Murphy, DeAnna. Strengths Strategy. "Confident Vulnerability". www. strengthsstrategy.com/2012/11/15/confident-vulnerability. Accessed 16 Nov 2016.*

"Confident Vulnerability means: to courageously celebrate and embrace the strengths, weaknesses, and needs of self and others without judgment. Its message, simply stated is: I know what I am, I know what I'm not. Both are okay. (This message, then, leaves me free to also embrace what you are, and what you are not, without judgment). In order to be Confidently Vulnerable, you must find confidence in your own strengths, and make peace with the fact that your strengths need certain things in order to be at your best. You must also learn what those needs are, how to meet them through your own strengths and resources [which includes other people], as well as come to understand and be comfortable with your weaknesses."

If Confident Vulnerability sounds like utopia, it may be because it really embodies honoring yourself *and* others around you in the most beautiful way. Whereas "teamwork" sometimes ends up looking like this: If the team has success, members are vying for the position of "most valuable player." If the team fails, the members look to see who they can blame.

What if we could just be upfront about what we are, what we're not (with openness to grow and learn), while seeking out the best in others and not needing to feel threatened or "less than" if someone gets credit for their awesomeness?

Shoot for this in yourself and encourage it in the teams you're involved in. And recognize what gets in our way from realizing this synergy *today*—jealousy and judgment.

Jealousy & Judgment

When you compare yourself to somebody else, you are naturally going to do one of two things:

* If you think that the person is better than you in some fashion, maybe they're more successful, better looking, or 'lucky', you're going to be jealous of that person.
* If you think you are better than that person, you're going to judge them. You will figure out a way to put yourself above them. You will give yourself reasons why you are better than them.

Ultimately, when jealousy and judgment are at play, teamwork, collaboration, and an expansive mindset are virtually unattainable.

In an unforgettable moment in the 2016 summer Olympics, Michael Phelps swam voraciously toward another Gold medal in the 200-meter butterfly final. The swimmer in the next lane, Chad le Clos, was forever frozen in history by looking up at Michael as Michael took the lead. The meme that followed? "Winners focus on winning. Losers focus on winners."

Exerting energy, time, and mental brain power into why you aren't as "good" as someone else is futile. The resentment and angst that jealousy produces doesn't help you. It literally holds you back from taking your own lead.

I can hear you right now,

"But, winning DOES matter, Alissa!"

The Strength Theme of Competition is one that thrives on comparing and gauging position, and that's not a *bad* thing. Jealousy is different, however. Instead of looking at that person in the lane ahead of you in jealousy, cheer them on! Welcome the fact that you now have a worthy opponent to catch. Use their outcomes to know what is possible, find your own benchmark, and then swim in your own lane. Remember, you will always be a second-rate somebody else.

In the same vein, judgment is what happens when you place yourself above someone else. This is different than discernment. Discernment is making decisions based on your values, morals, and education. Judgment is viewing others as "less than" if they think, decide, perform, or live differently than you. The foundation of Strengths is that we are all wired differently, so we don't have the same strengths as one another. And that's a good thing.

Curiosity

Jealousy and judgment are rooted in a lack of self-worth. Once you can discover how awesome you are, you can begin to see others with the same awestruck wonder. Can't figure someone out? Approach the situation with curiosity instead of judgment or jealousy.

How do you move forward from a place of curiosity? Consider for a moment that, rather than looking at someone and making a snap judgment, you instead wondered about what they are bringing with them, what life experiences have shaped them, and why they are the way they are. What if you asked questions with simple curiosity? Trust me, it changes your entire view; causes you to ask different questions; and helps you to look at everyone around you with compassion, understanding, and gratitude.

Benchmarking & Pattern Modeling

You already know that comparing yourself to others too much is not helpful or healthy. But looking to others' successes and benchmarks is useful when setting your own goals. This is especially true when you are new to an industry or field. The difference is in the spirit behind it. It is, indeed, helpful to have a bar to shoot for. If you're new to a career, isn't it natural and helpful to ask, "what can I expect for results in the first ninety days or six months? What have others done before me?" From there, you can certainly set your sights higher, but the point is that you have a benchmark, a comparison, with which to start.

The other time benchmarking is helpful is in a healthy competitive atmosphere. For instance, you can create a game or contest in the office or with a colleague. Remember: It's just a game. The outcome should have no effect on your own self-worth.

Setting Yourself Apart

Setting yourself apart starts with knowing yourself really well. Yet, this is the part that most people overlook, because they often think they already know it all or that there's not much to learn.

You are not most people. Why? Because you're reading this book. You've completed the exercises in Chapter 4. And I'm SO glad that you did the work! Now it is time to take your new-found epiphanies and put them to work!

For you to play out and embrace your amazingness, to truly set yourself apart—there are four steps you'll need to take.

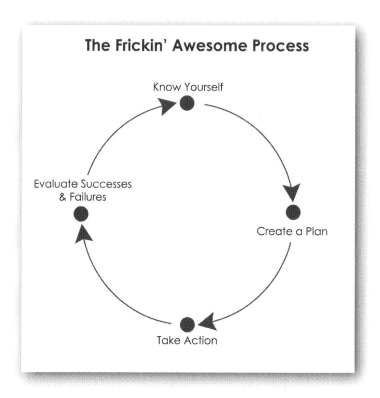

* Step 1: Uncover and deepen your understanding of yourself.
* Step 2: Create a plan.
* Step 3: Take action on your plan.
* Step 4: Evaluate your actions and outcomes.

Use what you learned in Step 4 to start the process all over again.

* Step 1: Uncover and deepen your understanding of yourself based on your recent learnings.
* Step 2: Create a new plan or tweak your previous plan.
* Step 3: Take action on your plan, and adjust your actions according to your previous learnings.
* Step 4: Evaluate and learn from your actions and outcomes.

Keep the process going! There is always something to learn, a new goal to chase after, and a new aspect of you to uncover.

Ready to Keep on Growing?

In the following chapters, you'll discover the best way to plan, take action, evaluate, and maintain the stamina to keep going. I promise you **every time** you go through this process, you will grow and achieve higher and higher levels of success. Planning, taking action, evaluating and learning will take on a whole new light. Take what you've learned and discovered about your awesomeness and apply it in the coming chapters!

Chapter 6

●　　●　　●

Naming Expectations of Self

You must expect great things
before you can do them.

MICHAEL JORDAN

Do you wonder why you don't get more done? Why others seem to get so much more done and have Strengths that you just don't have? Do you truly expect yourself to be superhuman? In all honesty, this makes you normal! But you aren't shooting for normal. In fact, 'normal' kind of drives you crazy.

You do not accept mediocrity. You *know* that you are capable of more than the average Joe. So why on Earth would you let yourself "off the hook" to accept mediocrity? You wouldn't. And you shouldn't.

But you aren't superhuman. You need sleep. You need to eat and drink. You can't live (and thrive) on RockStar energy drinks or coffee. You have human limitations. You're amazing and can achieve wildly phenomenal things, but you're still human.

Empowering Beliefs & Limiting Beliefs

Remember the story about Little Jack? Jack was dealing with a limiting belief that he was not smart. Like Jack, most of your lifelong beliefs are created by the age of seven. As new information and new experiences come in, your brain seeks to assign meaning and categorize them. Your brain would rather assign a negative meaning than no meaning at all.

Empowering beliefs, on the other hand, are beliefs that propel you forward, that positively affect your actions and your life. It's time you start racking up more of those!

Even if you had an amazing and empowering childhood, you still have a host of limiting beliefs. You can't overcome them until you know they are there. Once you identify them, it's extremely difficult to uninstall them especially if they are deep-seated. When you do overcome one, you have to replace it with another belief (ideally an empowering belief, right?).

No matter how aware and enlightened we become, none of us will ever fully arrive. What would be the fun in arriving, anyway? Life is about the journey and about achieving new heights. How boring life would be if we had nothing left to uncover and nothing more to achieve.

Awareness

Imagine you have just completed the best first round of uncovering your best you. Each time you move through the four steps laid out in this book, you'll expand your knowledge and understanding of you, which means that you'll be better equipped to be even more successful and even more frickin' awesome in the next round. Here's why. No matter how much we know, there's so much more we *don't* know. So the saying goes, "The older I get, the less I know."

Let me introduce the Johari window.[10] In 1955, two psychologist researchers at UCLA, Joseph Luft and Harry Ingham, developed this concept as a tool for illustrating and improving self-awareness and a mutual understanding between individuals within a group. I first learned of this concept when

---

10 *Luft, J.; Ingham, H. (1955). "The Johari window, a graphic model of interpersonal awareness". Proceedings of the western training laboratory in group development. Los Angeles: University of California, Los Angeles.*

I was in nursing school. What a simple way to begin to have compassion for oneself and for others!

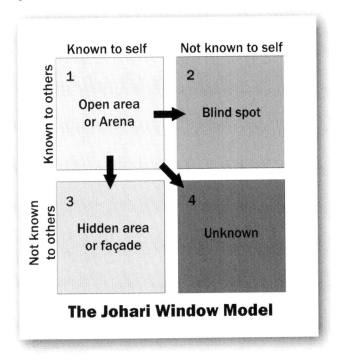

The Johari Window Model

To truly set yourself apart, you must *expand* your awareness. Here is how you do it through the Johari Window model. The goal is to stretch the "Open Area" wider and wider.

* First, you grow confidence by letting more people see how great you are with what you already know (from region 1 to region 3).

* Next, you learn about yourself by asking others what they see in you (from region 1 to region 2).
* Finally, as you evaluate yourself out loud *with* others, you expand into unknown areas of yourself (from region 1 to region 4).

Every "Frickin' Awesome" cycle widens your Open Area (region 1), which is when you truly get to start setting yourself apart.

Chapter 7

● ● ●

Growing Through Strengths to Become a More Awesome You

The person born with a talent they
are meant to use will find their
greatest happiness in using it.

JOHANN WOLFGANG VON GOETHE

As you grow your awareness of *and* your confidence in who you are, you will begin to optimize your Strengths. You will uncover your limiting beliefs. Your light will begin to shine brighter from within. You will spend more time in your Zone of Genius.

The one question at the core of growth, however, is this:

Are you willing to give up comfort to become great?

You picked up this book, which means you want to get out of a perpetual place of frustration and live out being the awesome person you are meant to be. Are you willing to do the work that's necessary to get there?

The thing is, as you turn on the lights in the proverbial room, you may realize that the room is pretty messy. Thankfully that scary Boogeyman in the corner is actually just a big pile of clothes. But, the clothes are dirty, smelly, and will take you a while to clean up.

A majority of people will choose to keep the lights off. They realize if they *knew* what was in that dark room, they would then have a responsibility to do something about it. The flaw in that logic, however, is that whether they choose ignorance or not, the mess is still theirs. That mess impedes their ability to fulfill their potential. I want more for you than that. I know you do, too.

The "Stuck" Space

Running a business day-in and day-out is not easy. No matter how many tasks you check off your list, the list never seems to end. And no matter how fast you feel like you're moving, there are times when you just get stuck. Your best-laid plan seems completely unachievable. You lose your way. It can feel like you're simply a hamster on a wheel—moving, moving, moving, yet going nowhere. You start to wonder whether there is any light at the end of the tunnel.

You might find yourself on your knees—possibly for the first time since the last time you felt this way—praying for a miracle. Perhaps you are hoping that some miraculous or magical windfall comes. You. Feel. Stuck.

Know You Aren't Alone

The stuck space isn't where only "lazy" people go. But it is easy to judge yourself, especially when you're in this stuck space. It's easy to berate yourself for your seeming inability to pull yourself up by your bootstraps and get into action.

Even though you know you need to get out of this space, you feel frozen. You feel foggy. You feel lost. You feel … hopeless.

How do I know this pattern so well? Simply put, I've been there, more than once. (More times than I can count, actually!) And I know the answer isn't just to "snap out of it" or "shake it off." (Isn't that the most irritating advice to hear when you finally tell someone where you're at?)

To navigate out of this dark place, it helps to understand why and how you got there and where "there" actually is. As you go into planning, action, and evaluation, remember this: The earlier you can identify the cause, known as a trigger, the faster you can navigate out of it.

Triggers: The Cause of Getting Stuck

We all have Strengths that provide our unique lens through which we see the world. Our Top 5 Strengths are our easy buttons, areas that we have a knack for. Each Strength has its own needs, contributions, and triggers. It is the triggers that send you into the stuck space. And what triggers you may not trigger someone else.

Have you ever wondered why someone got upset about something that would be no big deal to you? Or have you been accused of being oversensitive when you got upset about something that someone else thought was no big deal? These are clear examples of different triggers for different people.

You often can feel when you have been triggered. Common reactions to triggers are frustration, irritation, or even anger and rage. When we are triggered, like the turning on of a light switch, we are immediately pulled into the reality of Dependence—the stuck space.

For example, a trigger for the Strength of Activator is inaction or being expected to do the same-old, same-old. (Activators need to move and do things!) If a project that you're working on gets put on hold, or you have a barrier that is requiring you to pause, this will trigger your Activator. And that can thrust you right into the stuck space.

Toxic Triangle

I learned the concept of the Toxic Triangle from my mentor, DeAnna Murphy.[11] It was incredibly freeing to learn that, while it's frustrating and deflating to find myself in a bad place, there were reasons for it. Knowing those reasons gave me back my power and self-control. I hope you feel as empowered as I did learning this. Dependence isn't the only awful-feeling, non-productive, so-crabby-even-coffee-isn't-working-this-morning place you might find yourself in. There are actually three places (hence the term "triangle").

Dependence: The stuck-hopeless-please-someone-save-me space is called Dependence. In a nutshell, this is a place where the underlying feeling is "you serve me" or "you save me" (because I don't have the known ability to serve/help myself or others). This place is one of waiting … and waiting … and even more waiting. Racing minds, massive worry, and anxiety exist here, but not action.

11 Murphy, DeAnna. Strengths Strategy. "Moving Toward Interdependence--Through Strengths". www.strengthsstrategy.com/2012/11/07/moving-toward-interdependence-through-strengths/ Accessed 20 Feb 2017.

The frustrating part is that when you're in this space, it truly feels like your feet are in cement. The fear can be gripping. You know you don't want to be or stay in this place, yet you cannot move. You'll find yourself praying for a miracle, but not really believing it will come. The future may loom gray and fuzzy.

Independence: This is the toxic place that steamrolls, acts alone, and disregards others. You might find yourself saying, "If I want it done right, I just have to do it myself!" Or you might find yourself literally or figuratively pushing people out of your way, being abrupt or rude, and thinking everyone around you is just plain stupid. This place is self-serving. You may tell yourself, "You know what, I've got to look out for #1, because clearly no one else is looking out for me!" People find themselves here when they are fed up, frustrated, and usually hurt because someone let them down.

Codependence: For some people, codependence actually feels pretty normal. It consists of blaming and criticizing; it is filled with transactional relationships. Those relationships look a bit like this: I'll help you, but only if you help me. And if you falter, our relationship is over. You will be of no further use to me. Or, I'll guilt you until you become useful to me again.

Some people visit the Toxic Triangle, and some people *live* there. Here's the thing, whichever person you are, you only know what you know until you know something more. Whether you've been living in the Toxic Triangle or just visiting it, let's get you out of there and living in your own Zone of Genius!

The Comfort Zone: Why You Might Choose to Stay Stuck

No matter which of the three areas of the Toxic Triangle you are in, you know the situation is pretty bleak, right? So why would someone choose to live in that triangle?

Simply put, comfort. Even if that space may not be healthy, helpful, or productive, at least it is a known quantity. You can anticipate what it feels like. Plus, you know what to expect; what if you get out of that triangle only to find that it is *worse* someplace else?

Fear and simply not knowing that there is a different way are two of the main reasons that people do not venture outside their comfort zones. It might be downright awful there, but at least it isn't risky.

The Panic Zone: Where You Wind Up After Taking on Too Much

It is easy to jump out of one extreme and into the other when it comes to the Toxic Triangle. For instance, say you choose to leave the Comfort Zone. You create a list of all the things you can do to reach success. But then you try to tackle all of them at once. When you push yourself just a little too far, take a risk that was just too large, or start to simply feel over-whelmed, shut down occurs.

This shift from one extreme to another is common. But it is not the only way. I encourage you to take a different path, one that will put you right in the middle of your Zone of Genius. That path will lead you straight into the Growth Zone.

The Growth Zone: Your Sweet Spot

With this book you are taking active steps to move into the Growth Zone. It's uncomfortable here, but wow, do you feel alive! You're taking risks, you're learning new things, and you're discovering you are capable of more than you ever thought possible before.

You know what? It's a bit scary in the Growth Zone. But, no worries. You know, no matter what, you will be okay. As the saying goes, "There's no growth in the Comfort Zone, no comfort in the Growth Zone." So embrace discomfort! *This* is where the magic happens!

Zone of Genius

I have used the phrase "Zone of Genius" a few times. So what exactly is it?

Your Zone of Genius is that sweet spot where your skills, talents (the things you're naturally energized and good at), and passions come together. Think of the times when this has occurred in your business. Write them down and seek out ways to do more of *those* things.

People in their Zone of Genius shine. Literally, their energy, joy, and expertise *exude* from them. You, too, can find your Zone of Genius. Once you do, spend as much time there as possible!

Softening the Sting of Weaknesses

So what do you do with your weaknesses? It's foolish to ignore them. You should not simply pretend they aren't there. So what then?

First, if you focus on and optimize your Strength Talents, you will conquer two-thirds of your weaknesses. Amazing, right? From there, lean into your confident vulnerability to ask for help with your remaining weaknesses. You can build a system to help you. Or, if you have a strong desire or need to learn a skill you are weak in, work with a coach to identify how the Strengths you have can help you achieve your new skill!

The best example I can give here is my own. In my profile, the Strength theme of Consistency is 34 of 34. As it sits at the bottom of my list, it is quite deep in my blind spot. For example, I don't even do my bedtime routine in the same order every night. Sometimes I brush my teeth first. Sometimes I floss first. Sometimes I change into my pajamas first. Sometimes I sleep in the t-shirt and yoga pants I wore during the day. (Don't judge me!)

My morning routine has historically been just as haphazard. There's so much I want to get done in the morning before the kids get up and sometimes I meander from thing to thing, room to room, thought to thought, not finishing one task before starting another and realizing I need to go back to the first task. So, for what seemed like forever, I *longed* for a consistent morning routine. But how was *I* going to do that? I mean, really, I *suck* at routines!

In addition to meandering about in the morning, I was spending more time than was useful trying to pick out what to wear.

"What's the weather going to be like?"
"What functions am I going to?"
"How many appointments do I have and with whom?"

These are all questions spurred from my Strategic Theme. Once I finally answered those questions, I quickly followed them with several more, led by my Positivity and Woo Strengths:

"What am I in the mood to wear?"
"Who might I meet today?
"What makeup should I wear to match?"

"What shoes?"

"How long will I be on my feet today?"

Then, one day, I had an a-ha moment! I was finding my-self triggered (irritated) by this process. I realized using my Strategic Strength in this way was a total waste of energy and time. I knew there was a way for me to accomplish this goal of consistency in the morning. I looked at the Strengths I have easy access to (my Top 5): Futuristic, Woo, Positivity, Activator, and Strategic.

If I wore the *same* thing every day, I could use that Strategic Thinking and Futuristic energy to make plans for the day; come up with ideas for solving problems for clients; dream and plan for the future; and brainstorm products and ser-vices. Now, *this stuff* is energizing! And now, I was driven to be consistent.

So you know what I did? I bought logoed t-shirts. From there on out, my work uniform became a long-sleeved t-shirt, with a logoed t-shirt on top, jeans, and tennis shoes. I was able to reach a *consistent* behavior through one of my Top 5 Strengths.

What Strength can you use to lessen the impact of a weak-ness? For instance, do you hate bookkeeping? If you do not have Analytical in your Top 5, but you do have Competition, try timing yourself. Make it a game.

Do what you can with what you have to bring energy and light into the tasks you need to tackle.

Take a Bow

Here we are, at the end of Chapter 7. You have discovered what makes you uniquely you. You are ready to embrace it and are committed to growing into an even more awesome you.

Stand up. Take a bow. You deserve a standing ovation! This is more work than most people ever do. So, truly, congratulations for making it this far. I salute you!

Let's make your own a-ha moments count. It's time to move forward into Step Two of this four-step process: planning.

Chapter 8

Planning Begins With Self Care

*Love yourself first, and everything
else falls in line.
You really have to love yourself to
get anything done in this world.*

LUCILLE BALL

You now know what makes you great. You are gaining clarity on what gives you energy. You understand how you give energy to others. But what do you actually do with this information? Determining what to do from here begins with creating a plan.

Planning for success starts with you. If you've ever flown in a plane, and listened to the flight attendant as they give the safety speech, you have heard the following statement,

"In the case of a loss of cabin pressure, oxygen masks will deploy from the ceiling. *Put the oxygen mask on your own face before attempting to help others.*"

I promise you this: If you put yourself first, in terms of what you need to be healthy, you will be more energetic, productive, and have much more to give to others.

Maslow's Hierarchy[12]

Remember how I assured you that education is never wasted? Well, in a previous career, I was a Registered Nurse. And I learned something so important there that I have worked it into my coaching practice: Maslow's Hierarchy.

Abraham Maslow was an American psychologist who conducted research on mental health, the human potential, human needs, and human motivation. Through his lifelong research, he developed the Hierarchy of Needs. The Hierarchy suggests that human needs are fulfilled one level at a time.

You are already questioning me about why I'm bringing this up. Trust me, this has everything to do with you embracing your Strengths and growing in your awesomeness. For instance, you may be visionary. Or you may have a great passion for helping others. These are wonderful and amazing things. But for you to do those things well, you have to first

12 *Maslow, Abraham. (1954). Motivation and personality. New York, NY: Harper. ISBN 0-06-041987-3.*

make sure you meet your physiological, safety, and relationship needs.

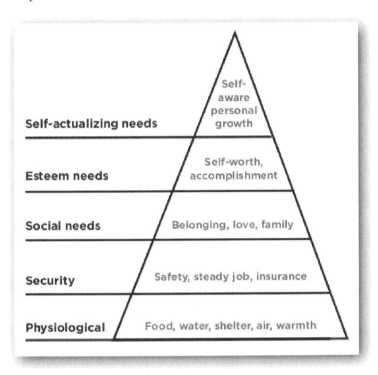

Physiological Needs & Safety

Sleep: We try to cut sleep on a routine basis, thinking *this* is the area where we can strategically find more hours in the day. But that simply doesn't work in the long-term. Might you short yourself every now and again and continue to thrive? Sure. But this is not the way to get "one up" on your competition. You'll harm your health and productivity. Want to learn more? I highly encourage you to pick up "Sleep Smarter," by Shawn Stevenson. Shawn knows his stuff and his advice is backed by science, not opinion.

Diet and nutrition: We also need to nurture our bodies with the right fuel. I'm not talking about any particular diet, but your micronutrient (vitamins, minerals, and phytonutrients) and macronutrient (calories from carbohydrates, proteins, and fats) needs do need to be met. Fad diets are nearly 100 percent unsustainable. And living on energy drinks, coffee, and fast food is a sure way to find yourself suffering from an illness or two.

Choose whichever diet (which simply means "way of eating") suits your needs, but as a former Registered Dietitian (yes, I was a Registered Dietitian, then a Registered Nurse … no education is *ever* wasted), I feel strongly about you not getting taken advantage of. There are a lot of people out there looking to make a quick buck on your desperation for a nutrition solution. The weight loss industry alone is an $8 billion-a-year industry. Please do yourself a favor and ask these questions when seeking diet and nutrition advice (whether by book, the internet, or hired professional):

1. What's the advisor's educational background? A registered dietitian or licensed nutritionist are the most reputable professionals and they are trained to help

and take into account other health conditions you may have. Go to *eatright.org/find-an-expert* for assistance in finding someone in your area.

2. Does this diet cut out a whole group of foods (for baseless reasons or reasons that have questionable proof)? If so, stay away.

3. Can you maintain this diet long-term? There is no "easy" way to health. If it sounds too easy to be true, it is. Period.

Exercise: This is the third leg of the health stool. You don't need to be a marathoner to be in good health. But multiple reputable sources, including the Center for Disease Control and Prevention, The Mayo Clinic, and the National Health Services in England, all recommend 150 minutes per week of moderate, intensity activity. That is just 30 minutes a day, five days a week. Pick your favorite activity, and go for it. Use a personal trainer, a gym, your living room floor and a DVD, or the good ol' outdoors. Just move.

In addition to the obvious benefit of weight control, regular exercise will stave off or improve countless health conditions and diseases. It will also improve your mood, boost your energy, promote better quality sleep, and improve your sex life.[13] And, guess what? You can make it fun!

---

13 *Mayo Clinic Staff. Mayo Clinic. "Exercise: 7 benefits of regular activity". www.mayoclinic.org/healthy-lifestyle/fitness/in-depth/exercise/art-20048389. Accessed 20 Dec 2016.*

Shelter and paid bills: This is an area many people take for granted. But the stress involved when you are living paycheck to paycheck is real. As you put in the work to set yourself apart and get ahead in business, make sure to track your income and expenses. Even if the numbers don't look like you want them to, knowing exactly what your numbers are is the first step to improving them.

Belonging

This level of the Hierarchy focuses on creating and maintaining good relationships and being accepted. As you give up judgment and jealousy, seek to find and respect others Strengths, and build collaborations and relationships that give everyone space to shine, this one is in the bag!

Self Esteem

This includes holding yourself *and* others in high esteem. And that's what becoming "Frickin' Awesome" is all about! You have made incredible grounds just by picking up this book and completing the exercises.

Self Actualization

The top level of the hierarchy was once considered something that very few people could achieve.[14] It includes fully accept-

---

14 *Maslow, A (1954). Motivation and personality. New York, NY: Harper. ISBN 0-06-041987-3.*

ing oneself, having one's full potential realized, focused on helping and giving to others. I propose that by using my 4 Step "Frickin' Awesome" Process, you will find yourself climbing all five levels of Maslow's Hierarchy.

Mental health: Maslow hypothesized that lack of needs met at various levels of the hierarchy could lead to illness, particularly, mental illness. While I don't believe the correlation is exactly one-to-one, this makes sense. Entrepreneurship is hard. There is the stress of uncertainty, a million things to do, and no one telling what to do. You have to create your own vision, direction, and prioritization.

What's more, entrepreneurship can be lonely. Incidences of anxiety and depression is common (although not always talked about). The less we talk about what's really going on, the more shame we have about it. Shame will never help you become a better version of you or thrust you forward on your path to success, so talk to someone.

As a former RN, I feel strongly about making mental health a non-taboo conversation. These diagnoses can be crippling and there are real physiological and chemical components that you need to address, sometimes with medication. What you decide to do from a medical treatment standpoint is really between you and your doctor, but I know you. You're not the just-take-a-pill-and-hope-for-good-results kind of person. You are *also* interested in doing what you can to take control and stay in the driver's seat of your own health and life, right?

In his book, "The Miracle Morning," Hal Elrod advocates six activities for 10 minutes each, for a total of one hour, daily to be successful. (If you haven't read it already, make his book the next one you pick up after this one!) Each of the six areas is important and hits on aspects of Maslow's Hierarchy needs. For easy recall and implementation, Hal created an acronym for the six daily activities that he incorporates into his recommended morning routine: **SAVERS**.

S = Silence (meditation)
A = Affirmations
V = Visualization
E = Exercise
R = Reading
S = Scribing (journaling)

This doesn't need to be a rigid morning routine. Find an option that works for you. Your mind, body, and spirit will thank you.

A note about other conditions that make you "different." Consider for a moment that *maybe* some degree of what is considered ADHD or Asberger's or "high functioning autism" is just different Strengths showing up. Maybe your brain is just wired differently than others. Rather than changing who you are, you simply need to surround yourself with people who think differently than you do and can support your areas of non-Strengths. And they need to surround themselves with the likes of you! I'm not minimizing the disruption or challenge of these conditions, but I *am* asking you to consider that because you don't perfectly fit the mold of what society tells you is "normal" also doesn't necessarily make you "disordered." Discussing whether diagnoses like ADHD are really a disorder and need medication or a gift that should be celebrated could be a book series all on their own, but as you complete and revamp Step 1 of your Frickin' Awesome process, consider all the good that comes from these conditions, too.

Taking care of yourself first may be the most difficult portion of the Frickin' Awesome process. Remember to be kind to yourself. Give yourself time and space to grow, making self-care part of your day-to-day life. When you realize you've been neglecting this area, take some time to put it back into your routine, which also happens to be the topic of the next chapter. Let's keep going!

Chapter 9

●　　●　　●

Creating a Roadmap

If you fail to plan, you plan to fail.

How have you planned your goals in the past? What systems have you used? I'm a firm believer in SMART goals. A well thought-out SMART goal puts you in the driver's seat of your target. It creates clarity, focus, and a clear plan of action. If you've never created a SMART goal or have not had luck with one in the past, *now* is your time.

SMART Goals With *You* at the Center

Setting SMART goals is key to achieving your goals. Create and write goals that energize *you*.

79

What are SMART goals? SMART is an acronym, which stands for:

Specific—You need to laser focus your intention.

Measureable—"Better" doesn't cut it.

Action-oriented—This is your "I will achieve ___ by doing ___" statement of your goal.

Realistic—If the first thing your mind says when you read your goal out loud is, "This is impossible," you'll subconsciously sabotage your efforts.

Time-bound—Where is the finish line? (For example, if you signed up to run a race, but had no idea where the finish line was, how could you target your training, your pace or your mindset?)

In the first part of this book, you figured out what makes you uniquely you and began to realize that the tasks, ideas, and approaches that energize you and drain your energy are tied to your Strengths. Use that knowledge to plan your SMART goals. (If the term "goal" makes you want to throw up a little, use "mission" instead.)

If SMART goals sound intimidating to you, or make you a little queasy, know you aren't alone. At the turn of this year, my friend had this to say about setting SMART goals:

"[Everyone is talking about] SMART goals... writing them down, mapping them out quarter by quarter in 90 day cycles... and I just want to THROW UP!

I am driven by my mission and vision, NOT by goals and money. Don't get me wrong—I want to achieve great things, and I do. And I want to make money, and I do. I just don't think sequentially, methodically or in any kind of organized fashion ... For me, goals are achieved when I dream about the things I want and need and think about the ways in which they might be accomplished. I speak them into existence by talking them over with people I know.

And often, I am surprised and delighted by what shows up and exactly how it all comes together in perfect timing and in ways I could never have planned. What JOY! My heart sings and I'm engaged and connected to life in ways that I cannot explain—especially to those who follow a certain path, one step at a time."

Even for my dear friend, who throws up a little every time she thinks about goal planning, SMART goals are a smart idea. Through them, she *can* experience joy. Who doesn't want that? But she does need to make her goal fit *her*. SMART goals can be driven by money or mission. Either way, your goals require action! Whimsical movement will rarely get you where you need to go, especially if you are responsible for paying the bills.

Take Action: It is time for you to create your own SMART goals!

Goals Exercise

Step 1: Start Broad

What areas of your life are you looking to improve? If you feel unfocused, there are six general areas that I recommend you consider. Write down what "success" in each of these areas looks like to you.

1. Business/career
2. Financial health
3. Physical health
4. Spiritual health
5. Relationships
6. Personal growth and learning

These areas will generally hit all aspects of your life. They are also intermingled; reaching a goal in one area can cause you to reach a goal in another area. Awesome! Conversely, if you focus on one area only and completely neglect another, you could cause pain, heartache, and losses you never expected. You'll feel "out of balance."

Step 2: Prioritize

Choose the *one* goal that is most important to you. (Remember, this goal will likely cascade into other areas.)

Step 3: Get Specific

Daydream what your life would look like six months or a year from now if you achieved that one goal. It might sound something like this,

> "My business being better in six months would mean that I'm not worried about how I'm going to pay my bills each month. It would mean that I have enough repeat clients to cover my expenses; each new client is a bonus! I will have peace at night when I put my head on the pillow. I will be able to take a Saturday off without worry that I'm going to regret it."

Look! Just like that, you have your SMART "T" set: six months from now.

Step 4: Measure

There isn't a lot that is measurable in the example I have provided. "Peace," "enough repeat clients," and "ability to relax on a Saturday" are all a bit vague. Let's dig in and look for what *evidence* needs to exist for you to know that you've hit your goal.

You'll need to make sure you are clear on what your expenses are. Additionally, you will need to know how much you make on average with each repeat client (especially if you offer a variety of products or services).

Also, what monetary amount makes you feel at peace? Is it $1,000 in the bank? $5,000? Or perhaps you think in terms of clients versus money. If so, what number of new clients each month brings you peace?

These answers to these questions are different for everyone. And, yes, they are often dictated by your Strengths, values, and past experiences. So don't get stuck trying to make this goal look like someone else's. Own and embrace who you are, and let that shine through in your goal.

Step 5: Identify Your Actions

Now that you have your "evidence" picture—the "S" and the "M" in SMART goal—how will you get there? Often the "M" ties to sales, revenue, or income. This makes sense, as you're in business to make money, and money is easily tracked and measured.

Let's say you have a six-month sales goal of $40,000. You don't have direct control over who purchases your product or service. You need to define the "A" of your SMART goal as something you actually have control over.

Continuing with the example, you know that you average $1,000 with each sale. This means you need to close 40 sales to reach $40,000 in six months. You also know that you don't close on every sales meeting. Instead, you average closing one out of every three prospects. Finally, you know you have to make 10 calls for every single sales appointment you schedule. Importantly, one out of seven appointments cancels. Pulling this all together, for every new client you acquire, you must make 35 calls and hold three appointments.

This example involves a lot of moving pieces with different numbers. Here is a breakdown to help you see exactly what you need to do to reach your SMART goal.

* To reach your goal of $40,000 in sales in the next six months, you need to make 40 sales.
* To reach 40 sales, you must hold 120 sales appointments.
* To complete 120 appointments, you need to schedule 140 appointments.
* To schedule 140 appointments, you need to make 4,200 sales calls.
* There are 26 weeks in six months, but you have a one-week vacation planned. This leaves you with 25 weeks in which to complete 4,200 calls. That breaks down to 168 calls per week or 34 calls per day.

Step 6: Get Real(istic)

At this point, you can now decide if the goal you set is Realistic (the "R" in SMART). If you find it challenging and altogether overwhelming to make 34 calls in a whole week, this goal requires tweaking. But, if you regularly make 25 calls per day, you could realistically stretch to your new goal.

Creating a solid SMART goal takes time. It's not just slapping an end result down on paper and hoping for a good outcome. Do your due diligence to make your SMART goal fit you.

As you begin to make a mental list of all the things that need to be done to meet your SMART goal, you may get over-whelmed. Don't. You've got this! To ensure you stay on track, complete Step 7.

Step 7: Task It Out

You know that mental list I mentioned? The one that includes everything you need to do to accomplish your SMART goal? Write that list down. Do a complete and total brain dump. Not detail oriented? Write down your ideas, then talk them over with a detail-oriented friend or colleague.

Yes, I know this can be daunting, but hang with me. Everything need not be done by *you*. Use the following high-lighter litmus test to figure out how to break down your tasks by responsible party.

Once you have completed your list, take out two highlight-ers of different colors. With your first highlighter, highlight the tasks that need to happen, but that do not *have* to be done by you. Ask yourself this: If you were a CEO of a large company, what tasks would you delegate to your employees?

With your second highlighter, highlight the tasks that aren't your priority RIGHT now. These are tasks that you will either put on a "later" list or eliminate altogether.

The remaining, unhighlighted tasks are those that must be done by you. With this list in hand, you can now effectively create a to-do list for yourself that you'll *want* to complete.

Do or Delegate?

You're a business owner. And we have already established that you're awesome. Now we need to figure out how to maximize your energy as efficiently as possible.

You may be on a tight budget. You need to be wise about the services and tasks you hire out, the tasks you ask a friend or spouse to do, and the tasks you do yourself.

Remember the first highlighted list? Take those tasks and write down how much time you spend doing each of them any given week or month. Next, identify how you feel when you work on those tasks. Do they drain you or do they give you energy? Do you look forward to them or put them off?

Rate each task on a scale of one-to-10, with one being "this totally drains me, and I'd rather poke my eyes out with kebab skewers" and 10 being "I love doing this so much! It wouldn't matter if this made me money or not, I'd do this for free!" If you scored something less than a five, it's time to delegate. Unsure if you can truly afford to delegate? Keep reading!

Delegation: An Investment or an Expense?

Ok, ok! I can hear you from here:

> "Alissa, I can't afford to outsource! I'm a one-man [or woman] show, and I'm struggling to make ends meet. I just can't do it."

Let's work through this together. If outsourcing a certain task will allow you to make more money, it's an investment. If not, it's an expense. Here are some examples:

* Spending money on an email automation service is an investment.
* Outsourcing your bookkeeping to a reputable bookkeeper who can do your books in two-to-three hours per month versus your four hours per week. Investment. (Seriously, that bookkeeper is saving you 14-17 hours each month, during which you can create more revenue. Bonus: You will rest easy knowing your books were completed correctly, which will help you immensely should you ever get audited.)

* Hiring a housekeeper every two weeks, but cleaning the house the day before in anticipation of her arrival. (Yes, this is a thing people do!) Expense.
* Hiring a housekeeper every two weeks and using the time you would have spent there to shuffle your tasks and activities to maximize revenue-generating work. Investment.

If you're strapped for cash, but you have a client that does something you need to have done, talk to your client about swapping services. Be sure to exchange checks to safeguard your business relationship and your bookkeeping, and call it a day!

Do you have a sister who is an accountant? Maybe she'll help you set up your books in a systematic way for free. I mean, you did let her borrow your clothes all through high school. Call in that favor!

What's important here is this: Money out isn't necessarily a bad thing if it allows you to make *more* money than what you spend. You are creative and clever. If budget is tight at the moment, find a workaround. Don't be afraid to invest in your business. And always remember to prioritize. Cut the spending on eating out or buying coffee at Caribou, not on delegating tasks that drag you down but are necessary to your business.

Chapter 10

● ● ●

Getting Into Action

*Don't be fooled by the calendar. There are only
as many days in the year as you make use of.*

CHARLES RICHARDS

You have identified what makes you uniquely awesome.
You have set SMART goals. You know what you want to
achieve and by when. To make those goals a reality, you must
put yourself to work. You must create and follow through on
actionable steps you can take every day to keep yourself on
track and on point.

Setting and Sticking to a Routine

We've all done it. We think that a morning routine and taking the time to plan our day is a luxury. You've got a lot to do today, so why not just hop in and get to it? Or, you stayed up late last night because, well, life. Sleeping in and skipping that routine won't hurt you.

But you also know this: By taking an hour in the morning to complete your routine (put the oxygen mask on your own face first) and plan your day, you will be enormously more productive, effective, and your best you throughout the day. You will be clear-headed. Rather than being at the whim of whatever comes your way, you will be in the driver's seat.

Stop denying yourself the benefits of setting and sticking to a routine. Not sure where to start? Here are two must-do's for your every day:

In the morning: Make it a priority to first take care of you in the morning. Then take 10 or 15 minutes to plan your day. If you happen to sleep through your alarm or your morning is thrown off due to the unexpected, take your 15 minutes at lunch. But do it every day.

In the evening: Take 10 or 15 minutes at the end of your work day or before bed to plan and prioritize for the following day. This is as important as planning your day in the morning. You tend to remember things you missed as you're winding down at night, so take advantage and brain dump those things into your planner for the next day.

Another advantage of taking 15 minutes in the evening is that you now have a few moments to review your day (because planned days rarely (if ever) go exactly as planned). Evaluate what derailed you, what took longer than expected, and what came up that needed your immediate attention. Could you anticipate those things in the future?

While it might be hard to commit to doing this, use your Strengths to help you stay the course. What energizes you? Getting to connect with people? Remind yourself that you'll be able to do more of what excites you if you've completed your morning routine. Hate doing the same thing every day? Do your morning routine in a different order or change up your exercise to feel fresh and new! Your morning and after-noon/evening routine should energize you and give you hope, clarity, and peace. Find your happy routine.

Thinking Beyond the Next Day

Routines can and should include tasks that you tackle on a weekly, monthly, and annual basis.

Weekly: Schedule a full hour every week to evaluate the week prior and plan for the week ahead. If you have a business partner or a spouse that helps you with your business, conduct a weekly same-page meeting (or Board Meeting, as I like to call them). Typical topics are activity check-ins. Are you getting accomplished what you set out to do last week? If yes, celebrate! If no, what can you do to get back on track or reevaluate the plan for the following week? If you work with a team, use a communications or project management app to keep everyone on the same page and to facilitate those weekly meetings.

Monthly: Schedule a minimum of two or three hours per month to track, evaluate, reflect, reprioritize, and plan the next month.

Time Tracking and Calendar Blocking

Each item on your task list will take time. You can chunk certain things together (like returning calls or emails) to be more efficient. You can also block time on your calendar for specific projects so you can treat it like a client appointment. Once you begin doing this, you'll start to get a better feel for how long different tasks and projects will take you.

When I started writing weekly blog posts, I gave myself 30 minutes each week to write. I never finished them that quickly. After several weeks of frustrating "failure," I simply began to block off more time. My expectations were a bit skewed.

Now I give myself two hours each week to write a blog post for the following week. If I happen to be on a roll and finish before the two hours are over, I will get a jumpstart on the following week's post.

Whatever your tasks, choose your top three priorities and put them on the calendar for the day. If they truly are your top priorities, they deserve time on the calendar.

Take Action: You are making efforts to set a new routine. Your routine will not become habit overnight, however. So how can you make the shift from "this is a really great idea" to "this is really happening!"? Take the next step and calendar it!

Calendaring Exercise

Step 1: Block Time

Schedule events on your calendar. This is a vital, and yet often-skipped, step.

Step 2: Set Reminders

Put reminders on your calendar events. Set a toned reminder alert. This will ensure you don't miss the reminder when it goes off.

Step 3: Allow for Grace

Be patient with yourself. If you miss a blocked time or two, simply restart them. Putting them off longer won't get you caught up. Every failure is an opportunity to learn. What can you learn about a new approach to these habits? All of these things will evolve. You're human. You fell down. So what? We all do. We all have distractions that derail us. Life happens. But let me ask you this. If your car ran out of gas on the side of the highway, do you just hitchhike home and forget about the car? No way! You may curse a little, but then you would figure out a way to get gas in the car and keep on driving.

Chapter 11

● ● ●

Handling Fatigue & Burnout

Great work is not ordinarily done in busyness.

ELIZABETH SKOGLUND, AUTHOR

Wow. We've covered a lot during our time together. We've added several items to your schedule that will take time:

* Adequate sleep (7.5 hours)
* 10-30 minutes of exercise per day, five days a week
* An hour-ish of self care every morning
* 15 minutes in the morning *and* at night for planning
* An hour every week to recap, plus time carved out every month

I'm betting you felt like you were already short on time when you picked up this book. How on Earth are you going to add *more* to that full plate?

Back in Chapter 2, we talked about the Strategic Grind. Remember that busy does not equal productive. Does the "stuff" that you're drowning in right now align with your best you (your Strengths and values) and *your* goals? Or have you taken on things that other people expect of you and fulfill *their* goals before your own?

Adding in the time to take care of you will help you get crystal clear on what you "should" be doing every day. Get ready to say "no" more often! It'll be hard at first, but then it will be freeing! As Steve Jobs said,

> "I'm actually as proud of the things we haven't done as the things I have done. Innovation is saying no to 1,000 things."

Still, at times, you will find yourself burnt out. Burnout happens when hopelessness and overwhelm rises. To try to keep up with the overwhelm, you begin to cut out what keeps you sane, balanced, and energized. You also continue to try to serve and produce, which now is coming from an empty cup.

Fatigue, constant serving, and giving isn't sustainable. And when you're on the brink of burnout, you cannot be your best self for your clients, potential clients, or family. The self-care I outlined in Chapter 8 does take more time, but … You. Are. Worth. It. And in the end, you'll be more productive as well.

Restart: Delay Doesn't Mean Defeat

When you realize you are out of sync with your Strengths and your goals, and you have put yourself and your health on the back burner, don't beat yourself up. Just restart. Even as I was writing the bulk of this book, I did this! I told myself that, "I'll just push through!" And, "A few late nights will be worth it." I gave up working out. I gave up sleep. I gave up my morning routine (because I was exhausted from staying up too late). I was 100 percent off-kilter. And it showed! I found myself emotional, physically drained, and mentally scattered.

Fortunately, I had amazing people around me that caught it even sooner than I did. One friend helped me refocus, reprioritize, and say no to commitments that I was feeling obligated to complete. Another helped me realize I was working against myself by staying up so late and reminded me to just go to sleep.

Look, I *teach and coach* this stuff. And yet I need help to see when I am sometimes out of sync. We are human, and we are not perfect. That is why we lean into our Strengths and surround ourselves with a supportive community.

So, again, don't beat yourself up for falling down or falling "off the wagon." This process is nowhere near linear. Just restart.

Chapter 12

●   ●   ●

Staying on Track

If you can't measure it, you can't improve it.

Peter Drucker

You have done such awesome work getting to this point! The key now is to stay on track. Even more, if you fall off track, you want to know earlier rather than later so you can adjust course.

Is Tracking Really Necessary?

Ever make it to the last few days before a goal is slated to be completed only to realize you are *way* off? If you tracked that goal on a daily or weekly basis, you:

a) Would not be surprised, and

b) Would have been able to course correct or modify the goal along the way.

Strengths Themes such as Analytical, Competition, Discipline, Responsibility, and Consistency can be energized by tracking. If you've got 'em, use 'em!

I….am not one of those people. Tracking is not fun for me and doesn't energize me in and of itself. But you know what *does*? Reaching my goals. So I am willing to track. To help me in this process, I am also willing to ask my business partner (who also happens to be my husband) for help (he has the Themes of Analytical *and* Responsibility in his Top 5).

Keep your final destination—your goal: **achieved**!—in mind at all times to encourage you. Write your goal down and post it where you can see it every day.

Sales Tracking, an Example

Remember the sales example I provided in Chapter 9 (the one on SMART goals)? To reach the six-month, $40,000 sales goal, we worked out that you need to accomplish the following:

* You need to make 40 sales.
* To reach 40 sales, you must hold 120 sales appointments.

* To complete 120 appointments, you need to schedule 140 appointments.
* To schedule 140 appointments, you need to make 4,200 sales calls.
* There are 26 weeks in six months, but you have a one-week vacation planned. This leaves you with 25 weeks in which to complete 4,200 calls. That breaks down to 168 calls per week or 34 calls per day.

Based on this, you have five numbers to track:

1. Calls made
2. Appointments booked
3. Closing ratio
4. Number of sales
5. Total sales dollars

Yes, all of these numbers tie to your single sales goal. Why? Because the more you track, the better and more accurate your goals can be in the future. You will also feel more in control and will have fewer days filled with hand-wringing, wishing, and hoping for that next sale.

How to Track Your Goals

What's an easy way to get tracking done? The sky's the limit! You need to find what works best for you. Is it pen and paper? Is it an Excel spreadsheet? A whiteboard? Would you do better with an app that you can use on your phone, tablet, and computer? Or perhaps it's an industry-specific tool that you already rely on for other aspects of your work?

Whatever you choose to track, stick with it every day. Engage a colleague or coach as an accountability partner. Keep yourself honest. Do not cut corners here.

Chapter 13

●　●　●

Taking Time to Reflect, Evaluate, and Learn

Learning without reflection is a waste.
Reflection without learning is a waste.

CONFUCIUS

Y ou have reached it: The final step in this process of uncovering and embracing what makes you uniquely awesome. This step is not the easiest, as it requires a fair amount of introspection. But without it, you will neither reach your goals or grow into your full potential.

It is important to reflect, evaluate, and learn as you go. You can work this process, in miniature format, into your daily, weekly, or monthly scheduled business sessions. Every quarter, however, you should designate at least one four-hour chunk of time, undisturbed, for this process. Once you complete this final step, you can then start the "Frickin' Awesome" four-step process all over again.

Take Action. Reflect on and evaluate the last three months. This is done without judgment, negative emotion or regret. You'll need your calendar, planner, and your tracking files. This chapter is chock-full of questions for you to consider. My hope is that they will spur you to ask even more. These questions are a starting place and, on their own, will lead you to substantial learning and leave you set up for an even more successful round of "Frickin' Awesome." Feel free to expand as you learn and grow!

Reflection Exercise

Question 1: What happened (both good and bad)?

That's a broad question, but review your calendar or planner. What things happened in the last three months?

* Did "bad luck" (things seemingly outside of your control) occur? Did the kids get sick and you fell behind? Was there a snowstorm that kept you from meeting an important client?
* Did "good luck" come your way? Did a new client call you out of the blue?

Dig deeper on your "bad" and "good" luck. There are usually decisions and actions that, if you look closely enough, *did* affect the outcome.

Look to see what "bad" luck you can anticipate and prevent, and add those things to your plan for the next quarter. For instance, if your car broke down, when was the last time you changed your oil? I once had a $2,200 repair bill on a vehicle I thought was in good condition! After looking deeper, the mechanic said it was because I went 1,500 miles over the recommended oil change mileage. The oil gummed up and voila. Bad luck? Well, not really.

For your "good" luck, look for ways you can duplicate it. That new client that "called you out of the blue," where did he find you? What made him call you? Ask him! And then do more of *that.*

Question 2: Did I follow through with my commitments to planning and activities?

Where did you succeed in following through with your previous "Frickin' Awesome" plans and activities? Where did you fall short? What got in your way? Did the plan simply not work because the numbers didn't add up?

For example, did you plan on getting up at 5 a.m., but aren't able to go to bed before 10:30 p.m. due to your teenager's homework and sports schedule? Knowing you need more sleep than that, how can you adjust your schedule so that you can give your body the rest it needs AND the prep time you need?

Question 3: Where did I get triggered (i.e, what frustrated me) and what was fulfilling (i.e., what made me feel good)?

Frustrations and fulfilling experiences. Remember that your Strengths have needs and provide contributions. When the needs of your Strengths aren't met and/or your contributions (what you have to offer) aren't accepted or honored, frustration and triggers occur.

On the flipside, when your needs *are* met and your contributions *are* honored and accepted, you'll feel happy and fulfilled.

When you revisit Step 1 (self-eliciting the things that make you great), use your frustration and fulfillments to lend insight into what:

* You need to ask for from yourself and people around you, and
* Things you need to do more of so you can spend more time in your Zone of Genius over the next three months.

Question 4: Did I reach the goals I set over the past three months?

Move through each of your goals and sub-goals. Did you exceed, meet, fall short, or bomb your goals? Also, were your expectations realistic when all was said and done?

Use the successes and failures of your goals to help set (or reset) your SMART goals for the next three-month cycle.

Question 5: Are the goals I set still the goals I am reaching for? If not, what changed?

Sometimes your goals change. Sometimes we just forget about them. I've found that when I make too many goals, even if a few of them are small, I lose track of them. Then

I find them later and realize they obviously weren't that important to me. Or I subconsciously lost track of them because they were scary and overwhelming and self-sabotage shut me down before I even started.

Question 6: Did I sabotage my success in any way?

What fears did you have going into this last three-month period? Did any of the fears come to fruition or hold you back? Also, when and where did you hit fear or other self-sabotaging behavior? (Having a palm-to-forehead, "WHY did I do that?!" moment is a pretty good indication that a self-sabotaging behavior occurred).

Question 7: Did I track my goals?

Did you track the way that you had planned? Were you tracking the right things? Do you need to track different measures next cycle? Did you neglect to track? Why? What held you back? Did you use the wrong tracking tool? Did you carve out enough time to do this well? Readjust your method of tracking to fit YOU.

Question 8: What obstacles did I face?

The more obstacles you can identify, the more you can anticipate and avoid potholes. This isn't the time to feel bad for yourself. Obstacles are not a bad thing. They are your best teachers. Once you have identified them, as yourself this question: can I avoid the obstacles I faced in the future? If yes, how?

Question 9: What failures did I experience?

What did you try that simply didn't work? First, pat yourself on the back. If you didn't take risks, you wouldn't have failures. There are no great accomplishments without risks and stepping outside the comfort zone. Next, ask yourself what you can learn from those failures.

Can't pinpoint any failures? Then it's time to up the ante!

Question 10: What things dragged me down?

The answer to this goes back to feeding the needs and contributions of your Strengths. If it sucked energy out of you, it may be time to take a new approach to the task: Delegate it or find a system or process to automate it for you. Ask whether there is a way to engage your top Strengths to create more energy around those things that dragged you down.

Question 11: Did I take care of myself?

Did you make yourself and your health a priority, or did you find it easy to push yourself to the side and attempt to "buckle down" in work? Please remember that you only have this one life and this one body.

Question 12: Who do I need to surround myself with?

What kind of support or expertise would have been helpful to you over the past three months? Who can you discuss your quarterly review with? Who's insight would be valuable here, as well as in the future?

Question 13: What else do I see?

Do you have any other observations? Is there anything else that sticks out to you? Use this last question as a catch-all to ensure you reflect on the things that matter most to you.

Self-Discovery Is Ongoing

Each quarter, you'll discover even more about yourself. What limiting beliefs did you uncover? What did you prove to yourself you could do that you never imagined possible? What patterns of behavior did you realize? What gives you energy?

By now, you *know* that you are truly awesome. This reflection and learning step doesn't need to come with guilt, shame, or regret anymore. This will be a time that you'll look forward to! And rightfully so. You get to reflect on how far you've come and plan the next level of greatness for the next three months!

Bonus Action Item

Once a year, take one weekend (yes, two full days) to get away from your business to think and dream. Reflect on the past year. I love doing this between Christmas and New Year's, but you can choose June if it feels right to you! Follow the same process as your quarterly reviews, but then take things up a notch. Zoom out and look at all you have accomplished and learned from 30,000 feet instead of 5,000 feet up.

An important part of Step 4 is reflecting and sharing learnings with another person. This person can help you answer the plethora of questions I provided for you. I recommend leaning on an accountability partner or other trusted and close relationship that has experienced the last three months with you. Remember the Johari Window from Chapter 6? Completing Step 4 with another person can expand the Open Area wider, shortening your own self-learning curve.

Chapter 14

●   ●   ●

People Matter

You are the average of the five people
you spend the most time with.

JIM ROHN

As you know by now, one of the base philosophies of this book and my coaching practice is that humans are meant to be in community. We are wired differently, each with our own Strengths Themes and skills. It's this way *so that* we need each other. We were never created to be "well-rounded" or "independent." We're not meant to function or succeed by ourselves.

The people you choose to surround yourself with, spend time with, collaborate with, and confide in are incredibly important. They can lift you up, help you think bigger, take bigger action, and thrust you to success. Or they can drag you down and kill your success and forward movement. Choose wisely.

With this in mind, it is important that we talk about relationships, especially those that are healthy and helpful, both for you and your business.

Collaborators

People very different from you in Strengths Themes, education, and experience are often the best of business collaborations. Who are the people that complement who you are? They are not always the people that make you feel warm and fuzzy. In fact, they may push your buttons and frustrate you at times. What matters here, however, is that your collaborators are in alignment with your values and end-goal.

As you interview consultants or other collaboration partners, take the time to vet out their professional values and be clear about your end-goal before diving in.

Accountability Partners

There is power in taking the SMART goals you created and sharing them with another person who is willing to hold you accountable to them. It may very well be in your nature to let yourself down more quickly than you will let others down.

Even without a "consequence" to your agreement with your accountability partner, your chances of following through are substantially higher.

If you're ready to "put your money where your mouth is," take your accountability partnership further. Write your accountability partner a check for $1,000. He or she must then promise to cash the check if you fail to follow through. This will certainly increase your chances of success!

Take a moment to join the Maximize Your Strengths Community on Facebook alissadairenelson.com/mys. Reach out there to ask for an accountability partner! Together, you can set the parameters for accountability (from a daily phone call or text to a weekly "report in" to other accountability measures) and create complementary relationships that will support you in reaching your goals!

Mentors & Coaches

There is so much value in hiring a coach who fits your needs, can pull the best out of you, and who asks really good questions. Additionally, having an objective outside party who will help you to see blind spots and look deeper is powerful.

Bringing up that Johari Window again! You expand what you and others see in you through conversation and discovery with *others*. Stretch your self-awareness and knowledge faster and with intention. Work closely with a coach or mentor in deep discussion. Doing this with others who believe in you and want success for you is vital to your success.

Mastermind Groups

Have you been introduced to a mastermind group yet? If not, now may be the time for you to join one. A great mastermind group is composed of individuals who bring support, differing Strengths, areas of expertise, varied backgrounds, and a full willingness to give freely to the other group members. Everyone involved, whether there are four or 40 people, is like-minded in the respect of what the goal is for the group. Find a group that is committed to massive success beyond anything any member has witnessed in the past.

A Note About Negative Relationships

There are times when you either need to set boundaries with certain relationships or leave them altogether. Is there someone in your life who is always negative, complains about everything and everyone, and yet has no interest in changing any of his or her own behavior? To protect your mind and future success, you must either significantly limit time with him or her, or you must stop seeing them completely.

You Are the Average of the Five People You Surround Yourself With. If one or more of those people are negative, look at life with a fixed-mindset, and always see themselves as victims, it is time you make a change. I know this is easier said than done, especially when it comes to family members and spouses. But some change is necessary.

You know how to view someone with curiosity and compassion now. Search for the Strengths and Talents, even in their rawest of forms, of the negative person in your life. By doing this, you may draw that person out of the Toxic Triangle simply by helping them see their own greatness and taking the time to understand his or her perspective. Have patience, compassion, and love for these people, all while you set appropriate boundaries. Never let anyone steal your drive or your dream.

In All Relationships, Let There Be Grace

With all relationships, remember that we are all still human. You screw up. Your business partner screws up. Your spouse screws up. Coworkers screw up. Clients screw up. Friends screw up.

The saying goes that we judge ourselves by our intentions and others through their actions. Work to have compassion and grace for yourself and others.

Take Action. Who are your five people? Take time to think about who you want to surround yourself with.

The Five People Exercise

Step 1: Now that you've discovered who you are, what you're not, and have embraced that both are ok, it's time to surround yourself with complementary folks. Who has Strengths and skills that you don't? Write those names down. If you can't pinpoint names right now, that's okay. From your Reflection Exercise, what skills and Strengths would support you in the next round of your "Frickin' Awesome" Process? With those articulated, you can start to *look* for people that have those attributes.

Step 2: Who do you respect, not only because of the *level* of success he or she has had, but *how* they've achieved their success? That is, who is successful that holds the same values as you do? Whose story resonates with you? Maybe he or she has had some of the same struggles you have. Whatever the case is that draws you to that person with such high regard, seek him or her out.

What can you do to get in his or her space more? If this person is someone you already have in your circle, simply seek out ways to be in their space more. Let them know how much you respect them and that you'd like to work and learn more closely from him or her.

Is the person you respect "famous"? Get on their email list. Do they have a book they've written? Read it. Do they host a podcast? Listen regularly. Do they have an online course you can participate in? Register for it. Are they available for hiring as a coach? If finances allow and you're ready to make a serious investment in you, hire them. Will they be at a speaking at an upcoming conference? Go.

Step 3: Find support. Who are the people who encourage you, lift you up, and who you have the same effect on? Do you have a colleague or friend that has the same challenges you do? Ask him or her to be your Accountability Partner. If you'd like a more formal (and effective) accountability relationship, hire a coach. There are lots of us out there, all with different personalities, specialties, and approaches. Find a coach that *fits* you. Here's an additional insider secret, hire a coach who is *equally* looking for good fit in his or her clients. A coach that takes on every client without some sort of vetting process should raise a red flag to you.

Step 4: Contact the people on your list, and make those relationships happen! Want to make a great first impression? While you can contact your people by email or by phone, you'd do much better by sending a handwritten note.

Chapter 15

● ● ●

Be Diligent and Courageous

I never lose. I either win or I learn.

NELSON MANDELA

Every time you repeat steps one through four of the "Frickin' Awesome" process, you will grow; learn; become more efficient; use your time, energy, and money more wisely; and set yourself further and further apart from your competition.

This Journey Is Not Linear
You will find success by diligently working through these four steps over and over again. Don't be afraid of failure.

Welcome it. Every experience, success, and failure is an opportunity to learn and grow. You may need to learn some lessons more than once. Embrace those, too. The journey of setting yourself apart isn't linear. Be sure to repeat your "Frickin' Awesome" Process every three months.

As we part ways (for now), I want to leave you with the story of Sara Blakeley, founder of Spanx, which is now a multi-billion dollar business. When she was a young girl, Sara's dad used to invite her and her brother to share their *failures* at the dinner table. Instead of being disappointed or upset, he would *celebrate their efforts*. Blakely said of the tradition,

> "What it did was reframe my definition of failure. Failure for me became *not trying*, versus the outcome."

You see, there is no such thing as failure, just feedback! What did you fail at today? Encourage risks and embrace failures. Don't be afraid of what you'll uncover and learn about yourself along the way. Remember, **you're already awesome**. Now go forth and share your awesomeness with the world!

Supportive Resources

Throughout the book, I mentioned many resources (such as the books, Sleep Smarter, by Shawn Stevenson and The Miracle Morning, by Hal Elrod) and want to support your "Frickin' Awesome" Process by providing you with many more that I have found helpful in my journey. In order to keep you up to date with the best and most relevant resources, websites, and products, I've created a page on my website, that I review and update at least once a month.

Check it out! **alissadairenelson.com/resources**

About the Author

Alissa Daire Nelson is a Strengths Strategy Certified Coach. She is the founder of Daire Success Coaching LLC and the "Maximize Your Strengths" podcast. Alissa enjoys spending her working hours leading business owners—especially married business partners—to greater success by eliminating limiting beliefs and helping them shine through their Strengths. She lives with her husband and two daughters in Shoreview, MN.

Futuristic · Woo · Positivity · Activator · Strategic

Daire2Succeed.com
StrengthsPodcast.com
AlissaDaireNelson.com

66118983R00083